FLYING BLIND

THE STORY OF A SECOND WORLD WAR NIGHT FIGHTER PILOT

In memory of my dad

with best wishes

Elizabeth Halls
née Wild
13th May 2015

FLYING BLIND

THE STORY OF A SECOND WORLD WAR
NIGHT FIGHTER PILOT

F/LT BRYAN WILD AND ELIZABETH HALLS

WITH JOE BAMFORD

FONTHILL

Fonthill Media Limited
Fonthill Media LLC
www.fonthillmedia.com
office@fonthillmedia.com

First published in the United Kingdom
and the United States of America 2014

British Library Cataloguing in Publication Data:
A catalogue record for this book is available from the British Library

ISBN 978-1-78155-345-9

Typeset in 10.5pt on 13pt Sabon LT Std
Printed and bound by CPI Group (UK) Ltd, Croydon, CR0 4YY

Contents

Preface

When my father died in 2012, he left three accounts of his wartime experiences: a contemporary diary, and two later, uncompleted attempts to write them up into a consistent narrative. This account is an amalgamation of these, and is essentially Bryan Wild's story as he wrote it, augmented by additional research by myself and Joe Bamford. Any historical errors in the main text, particularly misremembered names, or characters omitted who should have been included, may be attributed either to my father's lapse of memory of distant events, or of my own misunderstanding of his writing. Elsewhere, I alone am to blame. He died in 2012. Sadly, I can no longer check the facts with him directly.

This book is dedicated to the many fine airmen, from Britain and other countries, with whom my father felt it was a privilege to fly.

Elizabeth Halls 2014

Acknowledgements

This book was initiated and supported by Joe Bamford, and without his encouragement and knowledge it would not have been begun, or completed. My thanks also to Jay Slater at Fonthill Media, for his patience and support, and to Brigadier David Harris for his careful proofreading and helpful suggestions.

I am extremely grateful to other contributors for their help with research, notably:

Russell Brown for his extensive knowledge of all things related to 256 Squadron; Chris Eley for his indefatigable researches at the National Archives relating to 255 Squadron and the fate of Jimmy Ward; Brian Cull for researching and supplying information on some of the German aircrew involved in the Leros campaign incidents covered in this book, Alan Bodfish of the WO Bentley Memorial Foundation for the biographical details of Keston Pelmore; Sue Hayter at St Andrew's College, Ontario for records relating to George Reid; and the staff at the Library and Archives Canada.

For help with locating historic photographs, I thank: Peggy Sue Ewanyshyn, Sally-Ann Mowat and Alicia Odeen at the University of Alberta Libraries; Ian Proctor and Ellen Parton at the Imperial War Musem; and Lee Barton at the Air Historical Branch.

It has been a privilege to be in contact with, and assisted by the relatives of Bryan Wild's friends. I sincerely thank: Graham Berry (Joe Berry); Robert and Alice Wright (Roger Colley); Peter Crerar (Dave Crerar); Sharon Haggerty and Wayne Harker (Bill Cuddie); Ralph Gibbons (jnr) (Ralph Gibbons); Jennifer Chisnell and June Hollinrake (Deryk Hollinrake); Diane Tautari and David Hooker (Owen Hooker); Margaret Forrest and Katharine Fillingham (Doc MacDonald); Bronwen Hickmott (Keston Pelmore); Nigel Wills (Bernard Wills); and Tom Newell for making available Arthur Horsfall's diary.

My thanks to my mother, Bunty Wild, for her own recollections, particularly of Jack Barnes' famed party trick. Untold thanks go to my husband, Tony, for meticulous proof-reading and putting up with being a 'book widower' for so long, and to our dear Monica Newham, much beloved by my father, who so wanted me to write the book, and died the week it was finished.

1

Defying the Laws of Gravity

By the time Bryan Wild left grammar school in the summer of 1938, Austria had already been forcibly annexed to the German Reich, the civil war was under way in Spain, and Japan had invaded China. A few months into Bryan's apprenticeship as a draughtsman with Electricars in Birmingham, on 10 November 1938, the Kristall Nacht attacks took place on Jewish premises throughout Germany, Austria and Sudetenland, followed by the deportation of 30,000 Jews to concentration camps. These were not normal times; but Britain was not at war and Chamberlain was still trying to achieve peace in Europe. Meanwhile Bryan studied for Civil Service exams, aiming to take them in Manchester in October 1939. In Europe the months passed eventfully. Hitler dismembered Czechoslovakia and concluded a pact with Russia to smooth the way towards Germany's invasion of Poland. This took place without warning at dawn on Friday, 1 September 1939. Britain and France declared war on Germany on Sunday 3rd. Bryan never sat his Civil Service exams. Instead, like many other young men, he saw opening before him an altogether different life, and could not wait to join up and take hold of it—but he was not yet eighteen. He signed up at last on 3 June 1940. That same week Germany invaded France and Italy declared war on Britain and France. France had fallen before the month was out. The war was escalating rapidly and Britain stood alone against Germany.

Initial training: June 1940 RAF Recruiting Camp, Padgate, Warrington, Nr Manchester

I was young, but very keen. The medical was thorough, and during the lung test the Corporal had to bully me to hold my breath long enough to hold up the mercury in the tube. I was tallish, rather pale, and on the thin side. To my utter delight, the man whose job it was to gauge my fitness shook hands with me and wished me luck. I was in.

The date was 3 June 1940 and I was eighteen. I had to return to work for a short period, which couldn't go quickly enough for me, but on the 30th I was given notice to report to Padgate RAF recruiting camp near Warrington. I spent a month there learning the noble arts of drill, footslogging and fatigues, which made me feel rather glad that I had chosen the RAF rather than the Army. Exactly a month later I was attested, and became a member of the RAF as AC/2 ACH/GD U/T PILOT No 1057445, which translates mundanely as 'Aircraftsman Second Class, Aircrafthand/ General Duties, Untrained Pilot'.

On 27 July I was posted to RAF Finningley in Yorkshire where my duties were mainly on duty crew, flare path, and fire picket; for this was a bomber station with mainly Whitleys and Halifax. I was billeted with the station service police, but found them a nice bunch of chaps. I managed to learn Morse code in my spare time. I also had a narrow escape here; the first of many. I changed my mind in the last minute of accepting a flight in a 106 Squadron Hampden, which crashed near Scunthorpe. It is thought that the pilot lost control after being dazzled by searchlights on what was described as a Training Flight. All four crew were killed.

During August I was posted to Babbacombe recruiting depot on the south coast of Devon, prior to going to Initial Training Wing for aircrew (ITW). The place was crawling with RAF personnel, mostly young and untrained, like me. On our very first night, we were greeted with bombs, and one hit our billet directly. Fortunately, we weren't in at the time, but it felt like a near do. This was my first experience of the 'shrieking' bomb, with whistlers attached to the fins, and, boy, it was frightening. Every bomb coming down appeared to have my name written on it.

I was very aware all this time that a battle for Britain was being fought over the skies of south-eastern Britain and that at some stage I would be joining the fight. Like the others around me I was impatient to get on with the training and I was pleased when after only a week, at the end of August, I was posted to No. 2 ITW at St John's College Cambridge.

I had a grand time here. I found myself billeted with two others in one of the small studies usually used by the undergraduates, and we got along very well together. The College was a stimulating environment with its ancient academic atmosphere now invaded by blue uniforms of the trainee flyers. I was naturally thrown together quite a lot with two other chaps whose surnames began with W, because recruits tended to be dealt with by alphabetical order of their enlistment documents: Bernard Wills and Jimmy Ward. We were always grouped for physical examinations, and herded together when wages were being paid. We got along like a house on fire, and they stayed with me for some time to come. The atmosphere was cheerful and full of life. We had three very popular corporals to look after us all and morale was high. The food was excellent, which helped, and there were plenty of things to do in Cambridge itself: pubs, cafes and the Navy, Army and Air Force Institute (NAAFI), where we could eat out. We took part in all kinds of games, football proving the most popular. Physical training was not allowed to be ignored, and foot-slogging was also on the menu. Lessons here were held at various Colleges, mainly Magdalene, on subjects like armaments (Browning, Bren and Vickers guns), navigation and RAF law. In mid-September I felt I was in my stride and doing quite well with the lessons, although I found the gas lectures very boring.

Towards the end of September, the end of my stay at Cambridge was drawing near. The final examinations took place on the 1st October that would decide whether I would be suitable for flying, navigation or wireless training. I desperately wanted to fly and by the 2nd I discovered that I had passed. I had final interviews with the Commanding Officer (CO) and other various officers, and then learned I was to be posted to No. 12 Elementary Flying Training School (EFTS) at Prestwick, near Ayr in Scotland. If not yet flying, I was at least walking on air.

Aircraftsman Bryan Wild, Untrained Pilot No. 10577445, 27 September 1940, Cambridge. The white flash in the cap denotes untrained aircrew.

October 1940. Elementary Flying Training School (No. 12 EFTS), Prestwick, Scotland

Fortified against the wind and rain by my greatcoat, I walked towards the dispersal hut where I was due to meet my flying instructor, Sergeant Allan, of 'A' Flight, at eleven o'clock. I had arrived the day before with all the other aspiring recruits and had not yet been anywhere near to an aircraft. Atrocious weather conditions had cancelled all flights. I stopped for a moment outside the Nissen hut to view the grass aerodrome, my first opportunity to take in the vastness of the place. I had thought Bolton Wanderers football ground at Burnden Park was big, but compared to this it was like a front lawn. My first glance pinpointed all the main buildings such as the control tower, hangars, brick-built personnel quarters and section blocks. Apart from these I was intrigued by some other interesting structures which turned out to be protected dispersal bays for the aircraft, mainly DH82 Tiger Moths. These were single-engined biplanes, painted yellow; the standard trainer for all would-be pilots. Some were out in the open near to the flight hut, pegged down to counter the strong winds.

I opened the door and found myself in the well-lit main room where three other U/T pilots were lounging in wicker chairs. They turned out to be my close friends from Cambridge, Jimmy Ward and Bernard Wills, and a stranger, Dave Smith, a South African. I took off my wet coat and flopped into a chair, revelling in the warmth emanating from the cylindrical stove in the centre of the room. I had been in one other such Nissen flight hut before and this was much the same: curved, corrugated metal roof, metal window frames, the ubiquitous stove, desk, tables, umpteen chairs, and the whole room littered with the aircrew's flying gear, parachutes and other accessories. I wrinkled my nose; a faint musty smell pervaded the place.

I had hardly settled when a door opened at the rear of the room and Sgt Allan emerged in standard blue battledress. I had met him briefly on arrival the day before. Stocky, fair haired, rather fine features; about twenty-five years of age, I guessed. Allan called, 'Wild—I'll see you first'. He turned, retreated, and I followed. This room was small with a desk and a few chairs. As soon as we were seated, Allan smiled and said, 'Welcome to "A" Flight.' He paused to consult some papers. 'Now then, let me see. You spent a month at RAF Finningley, as an Air Cadet plonk doing various chores, and then you were posted to Cambridge ITW, where you were genned up on armaments, navigation, etc., before arriving here yesterday. Before I go on, have you managed to get home?' He glanced at the file. 'You live at Bolton?'

'No, Sergeant. Actually I've not been home since joining.'

'Bad show. Hopefully you'll be able to visit before too long. And your billet, Adamton House? Your first kip there last night. OK?'

'Yes, great. I slept like a log. And the food was first-rate.'

He grinned. 'You're lucky. Better than our mess.' He then selected some stapled papers. 'Right. Let's get down to business. Tomorrow the weather forecast is better. With luck we should be airborne. Read these. They're notes on the Tiger Moth and details of the course. You'll see that, weather depending, you'll be instructed with two or three flights a day. The rest of the time, mainly mornings, will be spent on ground lectures on such things as navigation, basic engine and airframe construction, cockpit layout, preparation for flight, and so on; it's all in there. This afternoon at two I'll be taking 'A' Flight, twenty or so of you, to the parachute section. You'd better get the hang of that. No pun intended. Any questions so far?'

'How long will the course last?'

'About two months. Again, bad weather would lengthen the course.' He looked at a diary entry. 'Your very first flight in this aircraft is at 2 p.m. sharp, but I want you here at one o'clock when I'll be showing several of you what makes this kite tick, so to speak. By the way, there are six instructors in each flight. You'll meet the 'A' Flight Commander at lectures in the morning: Flt Lt Gadd. The CO is Sqn Ldr Capper, AFC. You know what AFC stands for?'

'Air Force Cross.'

He smiled. 'Yes; not Association Football Club.' He then handed me a new log book. 'Stuck inside the first page you'll find the "Sequence of Instruction". There are twenty-two items from number one, "Air Experience", to number twenty-two, "Aerobatics". Keep all entries neat and all should be done in pencil until further notice. By the way, I take it you're fitted up with all the necessary flying gear? They kitted you out at ITW, I believe.'

'Yes, Sergeant.'

He stood up. 'Good. Be properly dressed for flying tomorrow.'

That afternoon, Ward, Wills and I had some fun trying on our flying gear, and then Wills forked out a camera from his kit bag and we all took some snaps. I had to smile as I looked at my two friends through the viewfinder. They were so different. Ward was sturdy and handsome. Wills was tall, and not particularly good looking; 'rugged' would be a more apt word. That evening the three 'W' pilots found out more about each other. At twenty-three Wills was the eldest of us, both Ward and I nearing our nineteenth birthdays in December. We all had connections in the North West: Wills was from the Wirral in Cheshire; Ward from Heswall near Birkenhead; and I had family in Lancashire.

Twenty-two of us on the course came from Cambridge. The other twenty-eight were Indians, complete with turbans. They spoke English very well; they were mostly the sons of India's rulers. We found them very easy to get on with, but they were all commissioned, so we weren't going to get much chance to become acquainted. A group photograph was taken of the whole Number 12 War Course, but I never saw any of these Commonwealth Officers again.

I had a pleasant evening at Adamton House, a mansion just outside the aerodrome where all the aircrew recruits were billeted. The dormitory, however, was not to my liking, double-tiered bunk beds and little or no items of furniture; but the lounge and dining rooms were warm and the food good. During the evening we all generally got to know each other.

The following morning there was a marked improvement in the weather: dull but dry with little wind. By midday my two friends and I were full of praise for the first session of ground lessons. There was a general eagerness among us to lap up knowledge of flight data. I was particularly enthralled with the first lecture on navigation, a subject I knew little about.

No. 12 Elementary Flying Training School, Prestwick, November 1940, with predominantly Indian officers. Bryan Wild, 4th left, third row.

Prompt at one o'clock, and complete with flying helmets, jackets and boots, the members of 'A' Flight were assembled around several DH82's with the instructors, whose duty it was to get across the first lesson of Elementary Flying Training, 'Familiarity with cockpit layout'. Sgt Allan was responsible for three recruits, Wild, Simpson and Woods, and told us to stand by the cockpit. He began, 'I hope you've all read and digested those notes I gave you yesterday regarding this aircraft. Now, stick your heads in there while I point things out to you. No, there isn't an elastic band from the propeller to the tail.' We grinned at that, and then he proceeded to outline the cockpit drill for the type and explained how the various controls were operated; how to use the parachute (there was one on the front cockpit seat), and gave us tips about abandoning the aircraft, adjustment of harness straps and using the inter-communication system.

Sgt Allan glanced at his watch. 'Right. It's now one-thirty.' He patted me on the shoulder. 'You're the first off. Be here at two and park yourself in the rear cockpit. I have to say it: don't forget your chute. We'll be in the air for approximately thirty minutes—in this kite, BB795. OK?' I nodded and was immediately aware that my mouth had suddenly dried up. The sky was now clear apart from a few clouds; a cold but pleasant autumn day. I noticed a skylark and gulped as I realised that in a short while I too would be airborne and defying the laws of gravity.

Just before two I put on my flying gear and parachute. While Allan was signing the Flight Record book in the hut, I walked out to the aircraft to climb into the rear cockpit and spend a few minutes looking round and getting used to the confines of the cockpit, as the Sergeant had suggested. I looked down at the floor and gently tapped it with the sole of my flying boot. God! It seemed paper-thin. Would I fall through? Would I be sick? I glanced along the wings: ribs, struts, wires, the gravity-feed petrol tank above and central on the upper wing. Up front, the nose and the large wooden propeller, leather edging round the top edge of the cockpit, small windscreen, smell of petrol and oil.

I suddenly felt uncomfortable, nervous and overheated: the fur-lined Irvin flying jacket was rather stifling, but I knew that once I was airborne the clothes would be essential. Even my hands felt clammy inside the gloves. I sighed, then looked down to the control stick between my legs. I held it gently and moved it to gauge its mobility. I noted with some satisfaction that the ailerons and the elevators moved up and down. I then tested the rudder bar: OK, too.

Allan climbed into the cockpit and adjusted the rear-view mirror so he could keep an eye on me. Almost at once he showed me how to use the controls, named the instruments, followed by some searching questions to me about my clothing, harness, parachute drill, the intercom and other important items. Then came the starting-up procedure dealing with tail-trimming, ignition switches, throttle, fuel and so on. The mechanic responded to the 'contact' routine and the propeller was swung. It fired after the second swing. I experienced immediately and for the first time the cool slipstream from the prop and instinctively brought the goggles down to protect my eyes. The engine was making a regular pulsating noise while it was warming up, and I liked the rhythm of it. We went through a complete cockpit check, a systematic procedure, checking instruments, controls, oil pressure. Then came the 'running up' and testing of the engine, and I noted that the control stick was right back into my stomach region in order to hold down the tail; magnetos checked, oil pressure tested again, throttle pulled back and slow running checked.

After a few final words the chocks were waved away and we were taxying out to an open space on the grass aerodrome ready for take-off into wind. I duly noticed the position of the wind sock. Allan had demonstrated how it was imperative to move slowly and carefully whilst taxying, and how vital it was for both of us to keep a watchful eye open for obstacles. Sometimes it was necessary to zig-zag in order to see clearly either side of the nose.

The aircraft finally came to a standstill cross-wind in order to view clearly the take-off path ahead. Then Allan called aloud the vital cockpit drill, remembered by using a code or catchphrase of initial letters: T.M.F. = TRIM AND TIGHTEN THROTTLE FRICTION NUT. M = MIXTURE CONTROL FULL RICH. F = FUEL: cocks on and contents sufficient for flight. (Later in my career I would add more letters to the code as I flew aircraft with more complicated controls, such as P = Propeller pitch, F = Flaps, etc.).

The aeroplane moved slowly forward and then turned into wind. Talking all the time over the intercom, Allan selected a point on the horizon in order to keep straight on the grass. 'We're ready for take-off, Wild. Keep your hands and feet clear of the controls. Here goes.' The aircraft slowly surged forward as the throttle was opened. At first the stick was held back, but as the speed increased the stick was moved forward to bring the tail up. I could now see ahead beyond the front cockpit and at about 60 mph we were riding on the surface of the grass with hardly a bump. I suddenly realised that my nervousness had evaporated. I was simply thrilled at this new experience and felt on top of the world even though we were still on the ground. I looked to one side and saw the parked aircraft, buildings, petrol bowsers flashing by. And then, as if by magic, we were airborne. Speed ... around the 70 mark. The climb straight ahead was gentle while airspeed was gained. At a height of 1,000 feet we levelled off and into a straight and even flight path. Speed ... around 100 mph. Allan asked me if I was enjoying it, and I said I was. I was surprised to find that I wasn't feeling squeamish in any way. From the beginning I had forced myself to look out of the cockpit to observe the ground below, but I had no feeling of vertigo. I was very relieved about this because I always experienced a sensation of giddiness when standing on top of a tower or high building.

For the next ten minutes or so, Allan gave me a potted version of the basic manoeuvres, mainly demonstrating the effect of the controls governing pitching, rolling and yawing. I was shown the effect of trimming the aircraft (i.e., balancing), how to hold the controls properly, and noticing the movement of the plane, particularly the nose, in relation to the horizon.

The instructor insisted on a routine to make sure who was in control of the aircraft. He shouted through the speaking tube, 'When I say "I've got her", it means I'm flying her. When I say "You've got her", you take over the joystick, saying at the same time, "I've got her." If we stick to that simple rule we'll never find ourselves in a bloody situation where neither of us is flying the damn thing.'

Allan then pointed out several landmarks, including, of course, the aerodrome. This prompted me to search for my map. I was fascinated by the panoramic view of the land below, a giant patchwork of greens, browns and gold, with rivers and the coast quite outstanding. Then Allan said, 'Well, Wild, that's about it for today. Remember I've got two other coves to deal with this afternoon. Tomorrow I'll let you have your first feel of the controls. So, let's take her down. Listen carefully to everything I say. In these early manoeuvres, landing the thing is the most difficult bit you'll have to tackle.

We turned gently for base, and soon, at a height of 1,500 feet, we entered the aerodrome circuit in order to execute an anti-clockwise approach. It was essential, Allan said, to keep a sharp lookout for other aircraft, and note the wind direction before descending to the true circuit height of 1,000 feet. On the leeward side of the airfield we turned crosswind to make the approach. The gentle glide and turn near to the edge of the 'drome was controlled by the throttle … at 400 feet, dead into wind with no drift. I noticed that there was little use of the engine; although of course, unlike flying a glider, it was always there if needed, particularly if the approach had been misjudged. I was amazed how silent it was. At 200 feet, the main sound was a faint whistling noise coming from the strut wires; at 100 feet, I listened intently as Allan raised his voice a decibel or two. 'Now this is the tricky bit … so watch and listen. We're coming to a critical point just above the grass … slowly does it … down a bit … about 6 feet is the spot to aim for … here we are … level off … I'm moving the stick slowly back … close throttle … this keeps the wheels just above grass until she's in a sitting position … she'll touch down any second now on three points, I hope … wheels and tail skid … There … there … she's down.'

I felt the stick kick right back towards my stomach and there was a flurry of rudder movements to keep the aircraft straight. It was a lovely landing. We taxied towards the waiting mechanics and eventually the engine was switched off. My first flight was over; all in half an hour.

On the way to the flight hut, Allan asked me if I had enjoyed the trip and also if, at any stage of the flight, I had felt sick or uneasy with the experience of flying. I was quick to assure him that I felt great. Indeed, I could hardly wait for the following day to arrive; a sure sign that I had most likely become hooked on flying.

From this day onwards I was in the air every day, but still doing ground lessons in the morning. I was instructed in several more main exercises, with emphasis being placed on items number 7, 8, and 9 on the list, which covered take off and landings, and it was during this spell that I became worried because I seemed to have difficulty in making a decent landing. I knew that some of my colleagues had gone solo on type in six or seven hours. I had reached nine hours and still had not mastered the landing technique. I became afraid that if I didn't eradicate this weakness, I would be removed from the course. The situation became so critical that Allan handed me over to the Flight Commander, Flt Lt Gadd, to deal with the situation. Gadd's first step was to assure me that with a little more concentration I would master it eventually. And so it proved to be the case. Two hours flying time later, after making good landings three times out of four, Gadd was satisfied. I went solo at the eleven hour mark, and after that my worries were over as far as landing the plane was concerned. Indeed, landing felt like a piece of cake from then on, and it seemed incredible to me that it had caused me such a problem.

During the next few weeks we were all put through our paces by covering every single item on the 'Sequence of Instruction' list; all twenty-two of them: steep turns, climbing turns, gliding, aerobatics, map reading, navigation and instrument flying. In my mind the most demanding manoeuvres were number ten, 'Spinning'; and the last on the list, 'Aerobatics'. The very experience of going into a spin for the first time was literally breath-taking, to say the least, but after several spins in both directions, left or right, I became used to it. It was vital that the pilot-to-be should know the cure. Aerobatics, too, was thrilling but tricky, and I felt that I would need a lot more practice with this aspect of my flying.

I had my final flights on the last day of November. The first was the flying test with Flt Lt Gadd, who passed me with some welcome words of praise. Then, finally, two trips that concentrated on aerobatics. I had completed 44 hours in all, half dual, half solo.

At the end of a course or on posting from a squadron, all pilots enter into their log books an assessment form signed by the Commanding Officer. This shows a summary of flying hours and an assessment of the pilot's ability. There are four grades quoted: A Exceptional, B Above Average, C Average, D Below Average. Sgt Allan jokingly said that there was an unwritten one: E Bloody Awful. I knew that there were very few pilots who were awarded the coveted Exceptional rating, but I hoped that I might receive the Above Average entry in view of the encouraging reports from Allan and Gadd during the course. But I was classed as Average, due probably, I thought, because of my difficulty in mastering the landing technique. However, I had no grumbles. Six had failed the course.

That same evening a group of us, who had all been successful in the flying test, spent the evening in a local pub to celebrate. Apart from Jimmy Ward and Bernard Wills, I had made a lot of friends on the course, and I was beginning to realise the true meaning of comradeship. We ribbed Bernard unmercifully as he had obtained the Above Average rating, whereas Jimmy and I had been assessed as Average. As the evening wore on, with beer flowing fast, the RAF mingled easily with some of the locals, and a competitive game of darts became the centre of attention in what turned out to be a rousing night of celebration.

The following morning proved to be an exciting day for the successful flyers, in spite of a few hangovers. We heard from the CO that all of us would be going immediately to Canada to start on the second course of flying, Service Flying Training School (SFTS) on Harvards. I had enjoyed my time at Prestwick. The Scottish civilians were very kind to us, the billet had been first rate with no shortages of food, and we enjoyed the local area. Most of our time in the evenings had been spent in Ayr, the ice-rink proving to be very popular. One of our party was an ex-Olympic skating champion, Maling, who taught us all how to skate. Even so, I left without a pang. Canada was calling, and I was raring to go.

We left the next day for a transit camp in Wilmslow, spending five awful days and nights in what we considered to be a real dump. After the luxuries of Adamton House the food and living quarters were dreadful. At least I managed to get 48-hour pass and visited my folks in Bolton as it was close by; my first break from the forces. Other chaps were not so fortunate and had to stick it out. My mother had died when I was eleven and my father had remarried and was living in Birmingham; my family in Bolton were my mothers' sister, Olive and her husband, Bill Lever, their son Roy (waiting to join the Navy), and their daughter, Pat. My brothers Alan and Frank also lived in Bolton when they were at home but were currently in the RAF on ground crew. My uncle and aunt were thrilled to see me, as I them. There was a lot to tell them all and I savoured every minute of

Bryan Wild with elder brothers, Alan, left and Frank, both ground crew.

my short stay. However, my lightning visit to Bolton brought home to me the hardships which the people back in 'Civvy Street' were enduring with rationing, blackouts and lack of transport.

I was soon back with the boys and on our way to Canada. We left Wilmslow at 2 o'clock a.m. to cause as little comment as possible on the move. The train journey took us to Guroch in Scotland, and by 11 o'clock on the morning of the 28th November 1940 we were on board the 30,000 ton French liner, *Louis Pasteur*, which had been converted into a troop ship. She was a large vessel, with one funnel, as I remember. We set sail in the afternoon and after five hours at sea I was sick as a dog and I stayed like that for three days. Our first night was spent on 'E' deck, below water level five decks down, in a room about seventy foot by thirty. In that room were eighty-seven of us, packed in like sardines. After that first night everyone decided that anywhere else in the ship would be better and for the rest of the voyage I slept under a table in the canteen. The food, too, when it could be faced, was pretty awful. One consolation for those who could still eat was that though the canteen food was not up to scratch, there were excellent rations available on board and one could get such exotic luxuries as milk chocolate. Some of my friends took it in turns to walk me round the deck. I survived by eating nothing but apples, the only food I could keep inside me. When I had recovered somewhat, we passed most of the time walking the decks when the weather was reasonable, or playing poker. Perhaps it was something to do with delayed recovery, but I remember that most of the time I lost. There were seven hundred of us on board altogether, all airmen. Fifty of us were untrained pilots. The Three W's, Ward, Wills and Wild, were lucky to be together and that made the trip pass much more pleasantly for me. We were accompanied by another fast ship carrying refugees to North America. There was always the threat of U-boats, but the ship was so fast there was little danger, and for some of the time we were escorted by the famous French submarine, *Surcouf*.

On my 19th birthday, December 5th 1940, I woke up to find myself freezing with cold. Outside the temperature was 20° below but we lined the side of the ship: we were entering Halifax harbour, a welcome sight. We had had no incident during the trip across and had arrived safely. Everywhere was covered in frost and snow, on land and on the ship. We docked at 11 a.m. and then we were lined up on deck to receive 25 dollars of Canadian money (4 dollars approximately to the pound). We were allowed to send cables from the ship to our folks back home to say we had landed safely: so much for secrecy! Complete with greatcoats, packs and kit-bags, we went ashore and waited in one of the large warehouses. Vendors selling coca cola did a roaring trade. In an amazingly short space of time we were hustled onto a special troop train bound for the Prairies.

The Three W's discovered our destination was RAF Station Moose Jaw, Saskatchewan.

The journey took four days, and what a journey it was, through landscapes of snow; lakes, fir trees, modern towns. A town called Truro in Nova Scotia was the first stop and we were astonished to find the whole platform lined with large baskets full of red 'Delicious' apples and local people handing them out enthusiastically to everyone on board. What a welcome! We cheered them to the echo as we moved out of the station. The news of our coming must have travelled ahead because other stations on the line followed suit. The reception at Winnipeg was unbelievable. Anyone would think Winston Churchill was arriving, not fifty unknown, untrained pilots. There were crowds on the platform, a band, flags and bunting, photographers—and even more baskets of apples. It was just too colossal for words. Here our party was split up: we pilots were put on a special train for Moose Jaw, while the others went on another train to Calgary. Our time on the train was memorable: marvellous food, good sleeping arrangements and wonderful scenery of mountains, vast forests, and the Great Lakes. To cap it all, before arriving at our destination, we were given a special dinner by the National Train Company, and boy, it was good! We eventually arrived at the small town of Moose Jaw at 7 o'clock at night. We had to stop and gaze at the brilliantly lit streets, a rare sight after the black-out arrangements back in UK. We had no time for sightseeing, however, because we were whisked away to the camp. The town would have to wait.

2

Wings over Moose Jaw

In December 1939 an agreement was signed by the UK, Canada, Australia and New Zealand to form the British Commonwealth Air Training Plan, answering to a desperate need to match the production of warplanes with trained airmen to fly them. In Britain this was not to be achieved by using the operational aerodromes under pressure at home. A similar agreement was set up with South Africa.

Canada was the primary location. It was not too far from the theatres of war, but provided dedicated aerodromes, ideal weather conditions, wide open spaces for flying unhampered by enemy action, and readily available resources such as fuel and industrial facilities in both Canada and nearby America for production and maintenance of aircraft. For Canada, this was seen as their major contribution to the war, and it was a huge operation, involving 94 schools in over 200 sites across Canada, nearly 11,000 aircraft and over 100,000 ground organisation personnel. Many Canadian young men also joined up to the RCAF and 55% of BCATP graduates were Canadian. Overall the BCATP trained almost half of all Allied servicemen in the various air forces, constituting a significant factor in establishing the Allies' air supremacy in the conflict.

Bryan Wild was one of over 130,000 air crew to graduate through the system in Canada.

1940, December, Moose Jaw, Saskatchewan, Canada, No. 32 SFTS

It was eleven o'clock in the morning. I stared out of the window of the lecture room to absorb the view of the aerodrome and the land beyond. It was something of a shock and none-too promising: mud and snow everywhere. The whiteness was dazzling in the sunlight but I knew that outside the clear air was bitterly cold. Even in the comparative warmth of the interior I felt cold, and fastened up the two top buttons of my greatcoat. I had taken off my special Air Force hat with earflaps, issued to me on arrival the day before. The room was full of pilots, all waiting for the arrival of the CO, Sqn Ldr Hannan, who was going to brief us on our immediate future. We were all very keen to hear what he had to say because the moment we set foot on the camp we had been informed that there were no aircraft for us to fly. The only aeroplanes available were two Harvards and an Anson. The aerodrome, with its triangle of runways, was situated just north of Moose Jaw, a small town set in the heart of the prairies, and linked east and west with other towns by the Canadian Pacific Railway and a main road. The land north of the 'drome was as flat as a pancake as far as the eye could see: no hills, no trees, no roads; a desert of snow. The camp itself was stark, with its outbuildings, four gaunt hangars, and flight areas completely surrounded by a barbed wire fence. We had slept well in our single-storeyed wooden building, a long room with two-tiered bunks lining either side, and having as a centrepiece a huge heater-cum-boiler radiating hot air in all directions: an essential piece of equipment. Though somewhat primitive, the accommodation was quite comfortable and on the whole we enjoyed the set-up. Two of these huts housed the pilots of the course, about fifty of us, and breakfast in the canteen had been excellent.

The pilots were called to order as Sqdn Ldr Hannan entered the room. As soon as everyone was seated, he stood by the desk at the front, with the blackboard directly behind him. He was in uniform, with the Distinguished Flying Cross (DFC) ribbon clearly visible just below the wings. He was aged thirty or so, with medium build and sporting a black moustache in his rather stern features. He took off his peaked cap and placed it on the desk. He talked for about ten minutes in clipped tones and with hardly a smile. The gist of his address was clear enough: a brief welcome; apologies for the fact that the Harvards hadn't arrived from the American factory—'but they'll be here soon'; until they came, extra lessons would be organised in that very room; we would meet our flying instructors in due course. They, too, had not yet arrived. And finally, he suggested that that afternoon we should wrap up well and wander round the aerodrome to get the feel of the place.

At two o'clock, that's exactly what most of us did. Again, it was a fine, bright day but terribly cold, and we realised at once why they had issued us with beaver hats, fur-lined gloves and special boots. We had been warned that venturing out without this type of protection could lead to severe frostbite, especially at night. The whole camp looked bleak and functional, probably because the buildings had been erected on a tight budget. As far as the eye could see it was flat, flat, flat. It was clear why the 'powers that be'

Moose Jaw camp showing large rectangular hangar.

From the air, the large rectangular hangars at Moose Jaw aerodrome are clearly seen. The photograph was taken by Keston Pelmore. *Elizabeth Halls in 2013*

Moose Jaw class room, lecture in progress.

had chosen the prairie sites to train pilots and other aircrew. The weather was excellent for flying (heavy snowfalls had finished by December) and the flat prairie landscape was of course free of obstacles. Furthermore, there was no blackout and so night-flying was easy to organise in terms of lighting, with plenty of runway lights and no problem in using powerful floodlights. The three of us stopped near one of the runways to watch a large machine equipped with giant rollers moving slowly along pressing down the snow. We nodded our approval; we had wondered how the loose snow was treated to allow an aircraft to take off safely.

Two main activities kept us busy for the next few days. Firstly, we soaked up all the learning they threw at us. Lectures in the mornings and afternoons turned out to be very interesting. Some of the instructors were civilians. Subjects ranged through navigation, knowledge of various types of aircraft engines, airframe construction, air safety and so forth.

The second activity was the most enjoyable of all, so we thought: as a result of the delay on the arrival of the Harvards, we had ample opportunity to visit Moose Jaw in the evenings, approximately five miles away. It was a small town, but most interesting and so different from the English towns we knew. There was one long main street and all the others branched off at ninety degrees. There were plenty of excellent cafes which cooked anything from steak and chips to ham and eggs, and also offered marvellous desserts such as apple pie and ice cream, which came

Tommy Hunter, Bryan Wild and Jimmy Ward in cold-weather flying gear, December 1940.

as a completely new combination to me. The shops too were stacked with goods of all kinds; no shortages here! We could get anything and everything we wanted, it seemed. After the austerity of Britain this was an eye-opener to us all. And open, free, ice rinks! Whilst skating at night under floodlight, I fell and knocked out a front tooth and damaged another, so I spent some weeks there without smiling! When I went to see the station dentist, whose surgery was in a small room in one corner of a hanger, I was alarmed to see that his drilling equipment was simply operated by a foot pedal like one of the old Singer sewing machines. We were also amazed to find that the river here had frozen hard enough to support a motor car.

By now we had discovered that ten of the twenty-two pilots at Prestwick had failed the course; the twelve of us left from Prestwick stuck together, but three of us became particularly firm friends—myself, Jimmy Ward and a Geordie, Tommy Hunter. We used to call him the 'Chinese Ambassador' because we thought he looked a bit Chinese, but he assured us he was English.

On the night of December 15th, the three of us met a small man in Moose Jaw in a large fur coat. He stopped us as we came out of a café and in a Yorkshire accent asked us if anyone came from the land of the White Rose. I told him I was born in Sheffield. That was good enough for him! He introduced himself as Mr Baxter, a Post Office worker, and said that he and his wife would be pleased to look after us during our stay in Moose Jaw. Before the evening was out we had been invited back to his cedar-wood bungalow and been introduced to his wife, his daughter Edna, her husband, Ed, and several other relations. There was a particularly pretty girl with whom Ward, at ease with any girl, had formed a firm friendship. On the other hand, I was a bit wary of the opposite sex, mainly because over the last few years I had not had much opportunity to socialise. And Wills was positively shy when confronted by some of the attractive girls who turned up at the Baxter's home during our regular visits to the bungalow. These kind people entertained us royally for the rest of the tour. They escorted us to local shops and cafes and generally took us under their wing. No one could possibly meet nicer people than the Baxters and Co. Many a night we spent in their house, singing songs round the piano, and always finishing up with an excellent meal. And Mrs Baxter *could* make Yorkshire pudding!

Although we had a good time when off duty, we worked hard while on. On 16th December, excitement in the camp knew no bounds as the brand-new yellow-painted Harvards began to arrive from America, and by the 18th, twenty of them were present, the total intake. And on the following day, the flying instructors arrived, all seasoned fighter pilots on a tour of 'rest' from the Hurricane squadrons in France. Most of them were officers, and they looked very smart in their fur-covered beaver hats.

My instructor was Flt Lt Miller, DFC, a Canadian, who was the Flight Commander of 'A' flight. He was tall and thin, and quite brown from living under a French sky for some months. I fixed his age at the twenty-five mark: a formidable figure enhanced by the greatcoat and beaver hat. At nine o'clock on the 20th December, the three 'W's, along with nine others, joined him in one of the two hangars to study the Harvard in some depth. Miller was clear and concise in his account of the aircraft's capabilities. My first view of the Harvard shook me somewhat. To start with I was surprised by the size of the aircraft, which looked large compared to the Tiger Moth. And this was far more sophisticated: a two-seater, single-engined (radial) training plane. The engine was a powerful Pratt and Whitney. The Harvard also had a metal variable pitch propeller, retractable undercarriage, brakes,

Harvard engine.

enclosed cockpit, flaps for slowing down the aircraft; and of course this was a mono-plane.

Miller then told us to sit inside the front cockpit (there were ten or more planes in the building) to study the instruments and get the feel of the controls. There seemed to be a bewildering array of instruments, but I realised at once that the main control panel of six instruments was the standard block which all aircraft would have as their central fixture— Spitfires, Hurricanes, Lancaster Bombers—all these had this panel directly in front of them in a central position in the dashboard facia, with other vital instruments (oil pressure gauge, etc.) on either side. The six instruments were: airspeed indicator; horizon indicator; turn and bank indicator; rev counter; rate of climb indicator; gyroscopic compass.

On 21st December, I had my first flight with Miller, and by 29th, and with six flying hours under my belt, I went solo on type. The difference between a Tiger Moth and this machine, I thought, could be likened to someone getting off a scooter and onto a powerful 750 cc motor bike: the gap was that great. I enjoyed flying the Harvard. It handled well and had no major faults in normal flying conditions. The view forward and sideways through the Perspex sliding cover was splendid. I had new techniques to learn, of course: pitch on the propeller; retractable undercarriage; flaps; use of oxygen; radio communication with ground control (radio telegraphy,

Bryan Wild in Harvard cockpit in the hangar, December 1940.

or R/T, as it was called), use of the gyro compass, etc. The 'Sequence of Instruction' format was roughly the same as the Tiger Moth course, but with some notable additions, the main differences being instruction on formation flying, more complicated aerobatics, and night flying.

As time went on, Bernard, Jimmy and I all agreed that we were very fortunate to have Miller as our instructor. He had four 'kills' to his credit in France, and I soon found out that he knew how to 'make an aircraft talk', as the saying goes, especially later when aerobatics was on the cards. The Canadian was very strict in his instruction presentation, and any pupil who was sloppy about a particular manoeuvre received a barrage of swear words over the intercom. I didn't escape some of this verbiage, but after a lesson, Miller was always quick to praise my good points.

In the meantime, Christmas came and went. From the middle of December onwards we had so many invitations to people's houses for meals over the festive season that I lost count. The Baxters invited the three of us on Boxing Day, because Mr Baxter was on duty on Christmas Day at the Post Office. Jimmy was already fixed for Christmas day, so Tommy and I were at a loss. However, the CO asked for two volunteers to be guests to a Mr and Mrs Coe for Christmas Day, to which Tommy and I duly responded. So on the day, we arrived at the Coe's with stiff collars, polished buttons, and polished faces, to be greeted by a very kindly looking Mr and Mrs Coe, an American couple, and a very pretty daughter, Mitzie Coe, who also had a very pretty girl friend, Elaine. Introductions over, we

Bryan Wild in flying suit, Moose Jaw 1940.

were soon made at home by the Coes. We got along very well with Mitzie and Elaine; it was all very satisfactory. Christmas dinner took place about 7 o'clock, with the biggest turkey I have ever seen, and possibly ever will see. We returned to camp late in the morning after a very pleasant party. Once we made friends with the girls in this way, we entertained each other very happily during our stay. The Baxters' show on Boxing Day was just as good, and after that, New Year's day was spent at the house of some of the Baxters' friends. There was plenty to eat, plenty of girls, and plenty of dancing. As I put in my diary, 'We had a wizard time'.

Right on through January and February we pilots were put through our paces as the flying training went on; navigation, cross-country flights, map reading, etc. There were several accidents, two of them fatal, all due to careless flying. Tommy Hunter blotted his copy book by selecting 'up' for his undercarriage after landing, instead of selecting 'up' his flaps. The plane slowly sank to the ground. It almost cost him his 'wings'. Bernard Wills got himself into a dreadful spin one day and only just managed to come out of it. As he stepped out of the cockpit after landing, the whole top metal surface of the wings had crumpled like corrugated iron.

I found formation flying tricky but exciting. Flt Lt Miller was an expert at aerobatics, and because he believed that a fighter pilot would only survive in combat if his knowledge of aerobatics was first rate, he went out of his way to teach me everything he knew: slow rolls, barrel rolls, loops, etc. I must have done quite well by the end of the course as he gave me a rating of 'Above Average'; a much sought-after endorsement. Only one in a hundred would receive the highest rating, 'Exceptional'.

And night flying didn't turn out to be as difficult as I imagined. I did my first night 'flip' on February 4th, quite an unnerving experience to start with, but after a few more trips I got used to it. As at EFTS, ground instruction was mixed with flying, and so it went on day after day. My last trip was on Feb 20th, a night flip. The same night, the South African Dave Smith spun in coming in to land, and was missing for several hours due to the blackness of the night. He wasn't badly hurt but was in hospital for 14 days, instead of going on leave.

One interesting chap I met was Keston Pelmore, who had been a professional photographer before the war in America, taking photographs of many famous people, big names like Count Basie, Fats Waller and Benny Goodman. He also loved cars, and had got up a members club for Bentley owners before signing up. He was quite a bit older than the rest of us, nearly 30, but full of energy and ideas. He took some shots over Moose Jaw and around the 'drome, and gave me copies. I was learning that in the RAF I would meet people from all walks of life and with a huge variety

Christmas Day fancy dress 1940, Moose Jaw aerodrome dormitory: Jimmy Ward, Bryan Wild and Tommy Hunter (probably taken by Bernard Wills behind the camera).

Bryan Wild with Mitzie Coe and Tommy Hunter at the Baxters.

Harvards in formation.

of interests. We had all been brought together by the war, and it was a unique mix of people that I had never encountered before in life. I found it fascinating.

We all qualified as Sergeant Pilots on 21st February. The entry in my Log book said, 'Awarded Pilots Flying Badge In Accordance with King's Regulations & A.C.1 Para 811, With Effect From 21.2.41.' It was signed by the CO Sqn Ldr. Hannan.

There was one strange anomaly concerning the course which no one in the pilots' pool could fathom. How was it that none of the Harvards had guns? As Wills said that very morning, 'How the hell are we going to shoot down enemy aircraft when we get onto ops? Are they going to issue us with pea shooters?' At one stage I did ask Miller the vital question, but he didn't make any comment at the time. So it was clear that all the pilots would be sailing back to Great Britain without having had a single flight with gun practice.

A new course was due to arrive in Moose Jaw at any time, but they were not ready to receive us at the embarkation depot. They therefore gave us money for fourteen days and free tickets to Montreal, where we were told to report on 9th March in order to catch a train bound for a transit camp in Nova Scotia prior to sailing back to the UK. This caused something of a stampede into town to spend the rest of our stay with the Canadian

No. 27 War Course, No. 32 SFTS, Moose Jaw: 'H' Flight. Front row: Flt Lt Miller DFC, 3rd from left. Back row: Bernard Wills, centre; Bryan Wild, 3rd from right.

Wings Day 21 February 1941. Dicky Bastow, Bryan Wild, Bernard Wills and Jimmy Ward.

families who had been kind enough to entertain us during the course. We had to say goodbye to the Baxters, the Coes and, of course, the girls. The night before the three of us were due to leave the town, the Baxters threw a party in our honour. We had our wings now. We had had our stripes sewn onto our smart uniforms and there were congratulations all round from a house full of young people very cleverly invited by the Baxters to form a good sociable 'mix'. It was a wonderful evening for us airmen. Delicious food, drinks galore, lively music leading to much dancing as the hours ticked away. I felt sad when, towards midnight, the inevitable moment came and farewells had to be faced. There were hugs and kisses all round, with promises flying thick and fast that we would all keep in touch in the coming months. In fact I kept in touch with the Baxters right through the war.

The day before we left, the three of us had planned out our fourteen days leave, which we decided should consist of four days at Winnipeg,

The Baxter family's hospitality to the airmen at Christmas: Back: Jimmy Ward, ?, ?Mr Baxter, Tommy Hunter, Bryan Wild. Seated: ? Ed and Edna, ? Mrs Baxter, ? Eileen.

four days Montreal, four at Toronto and a couple more at Niagara Falls. Somehow the trip was not a great success. Short visits to strange cities were a different kettle of fish to our stay in Moose Jaw with the jovial hospitality of the Baxters ever on hand. Even the much-anticipated Niagara Falls proved a failure. The falls were frozen, the temperature was 30° below and there was a hell of a blizzard, so we didn't feel too happy.

If truth be told, we were slightly relieved to report to the Regional Technical Officers on the 9th March, and be bundled into our train to Nova Scotia. This was supposed to be a temporary embarkation depot, but we ended up staying for five weeks all told. The food, the quarters and everything else here was awful; a sharp contrast to the comforts of Moose Jaw. Eventually, on the morning of April 13th we were posted to Halifax to board HMS *Wolf*, an armed merchant cruiser and next day set sail with a convoy bound for England. We were given a 'mess' on board with able seamen running the catering. There was an excellent canteen where we could obtain things cheap and during the voyage I bought lots of chocolate and cigarettes to take home. I didn't smoke, but I knew how well these would be received at the other end. We were not allowed to sit idle. We were put on 'watches' and had to man the machine guns at night in case of attack. Sports were held on deck once or twice, RAF versus the Navy: tug o' war and races—we did everything going to pass the time. Halfway across the Atlantic, the convoy was attacked by a pack of German U boats, and had to seek shelter at Reykjavik in Iceland for seven days. We had to part from HMS *Wolf* here. The camp Nissen huts were freezing and we slept in sleeping bags. The food was dreadful, all in tins. We had virtually nothing to do while waiting for our ship, except for swimming in the hot springs, which was the one consolation of the place. We did some of mountain climbing too, but we soon stopped that after being caught in a storm.

Finally, and very thankfully, on the 27 April, we boarded HMS *Royal Ulsterman*, a 30,000-ton liner, packed in tight as usual. After an uneventful voyage we came into the Clyde at 8 o'clock a.m. on May 1st, and what a fantastic sight it was for sore eyes. By a miracle it was a glorious day, and the purple heather stood out vividly under the brilliant sunshine. This really shook the Canadians who came across with us. They hadn't seen anything like this before. I was waved through customs easily. My suitcase was full of 1,800 cigarettes, twelve pairs of silk stockings, twenty pounds of sugar, ten pounds of tea, and various bottles of perfume, with other bits and bobs stowed in my kit-bag, so I was rather glad to get through unscathed. We were soon loaded onto a train which headed south for Uxbridge, a reception centre near London. Tommy Hunter was in a batch

Bryan Wild returning from Canada on HMS *Wolf*.

of airmen who were posted ahead of us, so our trio was broken up. I never saw Tommy again. There was a new foursome now: Jimmy, Bernard, Dick Bastow and myself. We had hoped for immediate leave but here for another two frustrating weeks we awaited posting to an Operational Training Unit (OTU). We had some hectic nights in London while the bombs were dropping. At first I was rather scared, but I soon got used to it. The air-raid siren went every night. On one day off I visited my Aunties Amy and Jessie in the South-East end of London. I got there all right, but as I was leaving their house at 10 o'clock at night, the sirens blew, and I hadn't gone very far before the bombs started raining down from all directions. I followed everyone down into an Underground station to take shelter. There I found the place full of men, women and children, some even sleeping there for the night. I was astounded at the cheerfulness and resilience of the people. After the raid was over, I felt my courage boosted by their great example. It took me a long time to get home. By various methods of travel, such as underground, taxi, tram and motorcar, I managed to get back to the 'Depot' at Uxbridge at 4 o'clock in the morning, feeling much the worse for wear.

We all clamoured for leave there; it was so tantalising to be back in England after all these months away, and not to be able to visit our homes. Finally, to our relief it was granted. I was sitting in the billiard room in the crowded mess one morning when West popped his head in and shouted, 'Everyone on three days leave!' I have never seen a crowded room clear so quickly in all my life. There wasn't a soul left on the camp inside two hours. Jimmy, Bernard and myself all went together to the north of England. Jimmy and Bernard lived in Liverpool, not that far from my home at Bolton. That very afternoon we were on the train again travelling north to Crewe, where we arrived at night, just as the sirens went. Here we split up onto different trains, but as my train drew northwards I could see an ominous reddish glow in the Western sky, and I worried about what they might find when they reached Liverpool. My fears were proved to be true: as we heard later, Liverpool had had one of its heaviest blitzes. I arrived at Victoria Station in Manchester too late to catch a train that night, so I waited in the YMCA until the milk train arrived at 5 o'clock in the morning. I arrived home in Bolton by 6.30 a.m. What a commotion that caused! And there was more pandemonium when I opened my suitcase and kit bag to reveal the goods inside. It was a wonderful feeling to be home.

After that longed-for spell at home, we had to return to Uxbridge for various examinations, interviews and briefings. Then, on the 9th May 1941, we all received postings to various OTU's, and I learnt immediately that mine was to No. 56 OTU at Sutton Bridge on the Wash in Norfolk. I was very relieved to learn that Jimmy Ward, Bernard Wills and Dick

Bastow were also posted there. To our joy, we learned that the aircraft were Hurricanes. We were allowed 48-hour leave to our homes beforehand. I had bought a second hand motor-cycle, a 500 cc Matchless. This machine was heavy and I realised I had made a mistake when I was thrown from it one day when the tyres got caught in tram lines. I decided to sell it immediately and to my astonishment and delight my elder brother Alan, who was there on a short leave, let me have his motorcycle, a 350 cc BSA (side valve). Alan was a RAF corporal fitter, who had no use for the bike because ground personnel didn't have petrol coupons. I did: one of the 'perks' for being aircrew. I felt I would arrive at my new posting in style!

3

Flying a Hurricane

The Blitz was already under way when Bryan Wild set out for Canada at the end of November 1940, just two weeks after Coventry's medieval cathedral had been destroyed in the bombing. He returned to England at its height. Under the BCATP scheme, the pattern of training was initially fast-tracked as the need for pilots during and after the Battle of Britain was urgent. Bryan Wild broadly followed this route: Initial Training School, 8 weeks; Elementary Flying Training School, 10 weeks; Service Flying Training School, 16 weeks. After gaining their 'wings', the pilots then went to an Operational Training Unit for about six weeks before becoming operational. Nine months after starting at Prestwick, Wild finished his training at 56 OTU Sutton Bridge, with 156 hours' flying under his belt. Towards the end of the war, pilots averaged 200 to 300 flying hours in training, over eighteen months to two years.

Bryan knew well that the Hawker Hurricane had played a vital part alongside the Supermarine Spitfire in the Battle of Britain in the summer of 1940, decimating bomber formations, and claiming over 1,500 of the 2,700 'kills' by British fighters in the affray. It could out-perform the German Me 110 fighter, but its effectiveness would eventually be overtaken by the German Focke-Wulf 190 and Messerschmitt 109 (F version) fighters, from which time it became more useful as a ground-attack fighter-bomber. At this stage, however, it still had a formidable reputation as a winning element of Britain's air fighter force.

May 12th 1941. No. 31 War Course, 56 OTU Sutton Bridge, Nr Kings Lynn, Lincolnshire

I found the Lincolnshire terrain ideal for motorcycling. The roads were almost empty of traffic and flat for miles and miles. The weather was on the cool side, with patchy grey clouds and occasional sunshine, but I did find it rather too hot in my greatcoat, leather gloves and flying boots. I pulled into a small layby near Spalding mid-morning to have tea from a flask and eat the sandwiches my aunt had made for me earlier that morning. I took off my flying helmet, greatcoat and gloves and enjoyed the warmth from a shy sun, while my mind dwelt on the host of events which had happened during the last few months. I glanced at my watch. I could hardly wait to get to Sutton Bridge, excited as I was at the thought of flying the Hawker Hurricane and I quickly mounted my BSA and set off again. Within half an hour or so I arrived at Sutton Bridge Aerodrome near the mouth of the River Nene which enters the Wash, and as I approached the guard room at the main gate, I was thrilled to ribbons as a formation of three Hurricanes flashed by overhead.

As I rode slowly towards the main building I saw a typical campus: austere blocks of plain brick, Nissen huts galore, the usual hangars and auxiliary outbuildings. There were no runways. I gulped. Tiger Moths on grass were one thing: Hurricanes were a different matter. I parked at the Sergeant's Mess, and once inside was immensely pleased to see my two friends, Jimmy and Bernard, at the bar. I joined them for lunch. They had arrived earlier that morning by train from Kings Lynn. Apart from the three of us, Jimmy informed me, there were five other pilots from the Canadian SFTS who would be in our flight. I also learned that at nine o'clock sharp we would all be meeting our Flight Commander, a Flight Officer Derek Dowding, at the flight hut on the perimeter. He was the son of Air Chief Marshal Lord Dowding, Chief of Fighter Command. For ages we talked about our recent adventures and visits to our homes. Then we withdrew to our dormitory to unpack. I had sent a suitcase of clothes in advance and was relieved to see that it had arrived safely.

Next morning, at the appointed time, a ten-ton truck drove the 'A' Flight group of pilots round to the dispersal hut. Once inside, I smiled as I saw instantly that this crew room was an exact copy of the one at Prestwick. The eight of us settled into the chairs and waited for our instructor to arrive. On the way over, we had noted with some excitement that there were five Hurricanes and two Miles Masters outside. The Master was a two-seater, single-engined trainer which was used for dual instruction prior to the first solo trip in the Hurricane.

The chattering stopped as Flt Lt Dowding arrived. We had met him briefly in the Mess the previous evening, and were somewhat surprised to see a younger man than we expected: about twenty-two years old. However, we had also learned from other sources that he was a fine pilot with many Hurricane hours under his belt. He was on the small side, but stocky, and seemed to wear a permanent smile.

He told us to stay seated and took up a position near the stove, rubbing his hands and generally taking in the heat from the stove. His voice was clear and pleasant to listen to. 'God! It's bloody cold this morning. I'm afraid you'll soon discover that yourselves here. This is the East Coast, remember. Fine in Summer, mark you, but sometimes...brrr! Right. Let's get down to business. In a short while, we'll all trundle out and clamber over the two types out there. We'll study them from prop to tail in some detail. Tomorrow, you'll take to the air in the Master. There are four other instructors, by the way—you'll meet them some time today. However, before we venture outside, I must tell about one or two precautions we have to take in the defence of this place. Because of our position on this coast we are within range of German aircraft. Over the last few months, we've had some scary intruder ops by their JU 88's—a few bombs, strafing and so forth. Not much damage, really, but we've had some casualties, and several planes have been put out of action.' He paused to edge his back nearer the stove. 'So, what have we done about it? We now have an army unit ensconced on a farm just outside the confines of the 'drome— Bofors guns, searchlights. But—and this is where you lot will come into the picture soon—to safeguard the kites from enemy strafing, we have a standard drill. This is what we do. At the end of flying just before it gets dark, a pilot flies a Hurricane to a designated nearby field to park it there until daybreak. There are several of these landing strips. Local farmers have taken down hedgerows to make the landing area big enough to land in. The next morning, another bod collects it. A truck ferries the men back and forth. Got it? Simple really, and very effective. If you happen to be detailed for this duty, you'll have to sleep here at this dispersal.' He pointed behind him with his thumb. 'There's a room back there with several beds.' He moved away from the stove. 'Right. Let's have a close look at the Hurricane. You'll all be flying in the Master tomorrow, so we'll have that out this morning. I suggest you put on your coats: it's a bit nippy out there.'

We all moved out to walk about fifty yards to a Hawker Hurricane, camouflaged in brown and green layers and the standard roundel on the sides of the fuselage: yellow outer ring, then blue, white and centre red spot; no squadron code letters, of course, because this was a training unit. I, and probably most of the others, had never been close up to this type of plane, and I was thrilled at the size and pugnacity of it. We stood on the port side of it and waited for Dowding to do the introductions. There were five other planes nearby.

'I won't keep you too long standing out here. It's too cold. When I've finished gassing, you can spend the rest of the morning studying the cockpit layout by yourselves. When you reach the time to go solo on it, an instructor will be with you to point out the controls or whatever, You'll probably know most of the gen about this kite, but nevertheless, it's my job to give you a brief outline of its specification. This is a Mark 2C. Single-seater fighter. I know I'm stating the obvious, but it's worth reminding you that there's no way you can have dual instruction on it. Someone will stand at the side whilst you are sitting in the thing and simply tell you what this and that does. OK? What else do you need to know about it? It has a Rolls Royce Merlin engine, liquid cooled. Maximum speed well over three hundred mph. Ceiling about 35,000 feet. Armed with four 20 mm cannon. It's worth mentioning here that because we are where we are these kites are always armed. Even during this course you could be called to do operational sorties if required.' We all exchanged glances at his blunt statement. He paused to smile. 'That's about it for now. I'll leave you now to browse. Be back here this afternoon at two o'clock sharp: the CO wants to meet all the new pilots; that includes the others in 'A' Flight. Tomorrow, as I said, you receive your first lesson in flying the Master. You'll need to be here at nine.'

I climbed into the cockpit of a Hurricane, No. 3205, where I had previously placed a parachute in the bucket seat. I had also removed my greatcoat. I wanted to experience a 'sitting' which was as near as possible to the actual thing. I closed the sliding Perspex hood and immediately sensed the confining limitations of the cockpit. I was surprised to see so many bars lining the hood, thus restricting the view. In contrast the Harvard had an excellent exterior vision. I didn't dwell on it; I was too busy taking in the stunning layout of the instruments and controls. There was the standard centre instrument panel, of course, but there seemed to be umpteen more 'things' to operate than on the simple Harvard.

I then held the control column. This was something very different: a small wheel-shaped grip at the top of the stick. Here, positioned within reach of the thumb on the right hand, were two buttons. I knew that they were the gun button and the camera button. I then looked up towards the nose, which was blocking all view forward whilst in a three-point sitting position. The small windscreen dead ahead was made of bullet-proof glass about two inches thick. Just on front of that, and fastened near the top of the instrument panel, was the gun-sight. Altogether there was very little sight of the sky ahead. For the next ten minutes or so I systematically studied the instruments and controls, moving from the main control box housing the undercarriage lever, pitch control lever, trimming etc., to the areas containing such vital instruments as petrol gauges, oil pressure, and oxygen.

The next morning I thoroughly enjoyed my first breakfast in the Sergeant's Mess. This was also my first introduction to the WAAFs, or Women's Auxiliary Air Force. They were serving at the tables. Up until that morning I had only seen them occasionally from a distance. They looked smart and professional. Like most airmen I knew, I respected them greatly and recognised the various and valuable roles they carried out. With the other two 'W's, I left the Mess to walk to the flight hut. It was milder and the sun was beginning to show. On the way, we recalled our meeting the day before with the CO of the course, a Wg Cdr Maguire DFC, a Battle of Britain ace. He had talked to us for about fifteen minutes. There was the standard welcome, but we were very impressed by his advice about flying the Hurricane. The gist of it was: treat it with respect; don't start throwing it about the sky until you've got the complete hang of it. He ended by informing us that there would not be any firing practice on the Course. That would come later if and when we were posted to a Squadron.

We arrived at the Flight hut at nine and were introduced to the other instructors. Within minutes pilots were being linked up with their respective tutors. I met Flt Lt Whitty: youngish, tall, pale complexion and wiry. He said, 'I'm your instructor for the course. We'll be off at ten sharp in the Master. You'll find it fairly easy to fly, and if I feel you've cracked it, you can go solo this afternoon.' This surprise announcement left me speechless. I had expected several lessons. Whitty smiled. 'After you've gone solo, you'll be able to tackle the Hurricane tomorrow. We need fighter pilots badly, you know … we haven't got time to mess about!' We both grinned at this. I thought there was some truth in it.

Later, when we were both ensconced in the Miles Master two-seater trainer, Whitty spent some considerable time talking through the cockpit drill. I found it was very similar to the Harvard layout. It only took Whitty forty-five minutes flying time to decide that I could go solo. The solo flight lasted for an hour and a half, and I found the aircraft delightful to fly. I was told I would be flying it a few more times during the course.

While I was in the air in this machine, I was wearing for the first time a Mae West life jacket. This floating aid, named after the film star for obvious reasons, could be a lifesaver for those who were unfortunate to have to ditch an aircraft or bale out of one when flying over the sea. I realised the particular importance of it at this aerodrome as I spent quite a bit of my time flying round the coast of Lincolnshire and Norfolk.

That evening, in the Sergeants Mess, the pilots talked over our experiences. Everyone had gone solo on the Master. Over pints of beer, we all switched our discussion to the prospect of going solo on the Hurricane the very next morning. By nine o'clock, I was feeling somewhat exhausted from the excitement of the day, so I retired to the quietness of the lounge to fill in my diary. I had started it the moment I joined the RAF. Some days I hadn't had the time to fill in the entries, which meant that I often had some catching up to do. This time was one of them. Apart from my own experiences, I also entered notable events from everyday news items from the newspaper or radio sources. I turned over the pages to glance at my entries from 26 June 1940, when I volunteered. I would have been called up anyway in December when I was nineteen, but I had been told that if I joined up before that time, I would stand a very good chance of getting on a pilot's training course. I wondered later if that had been a recruiting ploy to get early entrants. There had also been the inspiring example of Harry Goslin, the Bolton Wanderer's captain, who had made a rousing speech to the football crowd on Easter Saturday in 1939, urging those eligible to join up to do so. He and the whole of the Bolton Wanderers football team had then joined up en masse in the Army. I had seen many a game at Burnden Park and the Wanderers' example was a fine one to follow. I had kept it in the back of my mind.

Dotted through the rest of my diary were headlines I had written about the progress of the war: May to June 1940 was the Dunkirk evacuation and on 14th June the Germans entered Paris, while Italian troops invaded France. July to September 1940 saw the Battle of Britain rage over Southern England, followed by the terrible Blitz. From July 1940 to May 1941 the Battle of the Atlantic continued. The Italians made early gains in North and East Africa and by January 1941, Rommel was ensconced in Africa. I closed the book. I felt cold and dashed. It was all bad news. I tried to recall some of the stirring speeches Winston Churchill had made. Was it he who had made the stark and chilling statement that Britain stood alone against the might of the German war machine? I was suddenly annoyed with myself for being so morbid. I remembered that first London air raid I experienced at Uxbridge, with unflinching morale and cheerfulness of those taking shelter night after night down there. Here I was, wallowing in some form of despair, and yet I had all the comforts of this RAF establishment; good food and warm quarters, and fine colleagues around me. Moreover I was being trained to take part in the fight and it was easy to lose sight of that in the duration of this long period of training. A smile came as I remembered the piece of good news hidden in my diary entries: the Battle of Britain. The Luftwaffe had been defeated by the 'few', as Churchill had so succinctly put it. Inspiring names sprang quickly to mind, already legendary in the RAF: Douglas Bader, 'Sailor' Malan, Bob Tuck, 'Screwball' Beurling, Johnnie Johnson and many others. I straightened my back and headed back to the Mess bar. Within minutes I had joined my colleagues to sample more ale, the momentary blues behind me. That night I slept like a log.

The following morning, a lovely day weather-wise, all the pilots of 'A' Flight reported to dispersal for their solo flights in the Hurricane. I was one of the first to be standing next to the aircraft, number 4091. Whitty was saying, 'I see you've placed the parachute in ... let me check this.' He inspected the Mae West I was wearing. 'That's OK. You know the drill about its use, of course?' I nodded. 'Good. I see you've got the whistle buttonholed.' He touched it, attached to the top of my battle dress. 'Before you climb up: you know how to use the RT ... I'm sure you do, but I'll remind you in a minute of the call signs. Now, let's walk slowly round it and I'll point out a few things.'

Whilst we had been talking, I couldn't help but notice a swell of ground crews forming like a swarm of bees round the two dispersal huts where other pilots were receiving their briefings on the Hurricanes. Among the milling figures I could make out engine fitters, electricians, and men operating starter trolleys. There were petrol bowsers and various other vehicles. It was an exciting bustle of activity and it brought home to me again what a big operation surrounded us all and how vital was the role of these men. I thought of my two brothers, both ground crew. All air personnel were fully aware that the flying machines would never get off the deck without these men.

Whitty started his briefing at the wings and then progressed along the front of the aircraft. 'Note the navigation lights near the wingtips, and the landing lights in the leading edge. Two 20 mm cannon fairing in each wing; a variable pitch prop; long ailerons...' He moved forward to the fuselage. 'Sliding canopy, bullet-proof windscreen, aerial mast with line to tail stub.' Then to the tail. 'A fine tail unit. Note the small trimming tabs on the elevators.' He then bent down slightly to indicate the undercarriage fairing. 'Do you see that, Wild? The wheels retract inwards. Good, that; it makes it stable. A Spitfire's undercart retracts outwards.' He pulled down from the fuselage the retractable entry footstep near the tail. 'OK. Climb in and I'll come alongside on the wing to explain the ropes. I know you spent some time doing this yesterday, so I take it you've sussed out most of the controls and instruments. Don't put on your flying helmet yet; there are one or two things I want to spell out before you set off.' Once settled in the cockpit, I paid attention once more as Whitty went on. 'Cockpit drill now. I know you know it, but I have to go over it with you ... right? The drill is much the same for any aircraft. T.M.P.F.F. Remember these letters. Never start rolling forward for take-off until you've checked them. T equals Trim. Turn the wheel slightly forward to make sure the tail comes up. M equals Mixture. Push the lever full forward to make it rich for take-off; ease back when safely in the air. P equals pitch: prop to fine for take-off; lever back to coarse for cruising. Revs must be reduced of course. Double meaning for F: Flaps—must be up for take-off. F also equals Fuel: check that petrol cocks are on, and bloody well make sure you've enough gas to get you where you're going!' He smiled and gave me a pat on the back. 'Finally, S equals Sperry Gyro Compass: check your main compass, then set the gyro compass on that course. Only when you've gone through this drill will you make a second check on your gear: parachute and harness clipped tight. See that you're plugged in on R/T. The moment you leave this pad, contact control to tell them you're taxying out. Your call sign, remember, is 'Skylark' 26.[1] Ground control is 'Rosebush'. Remember the drill. If you transmit, you say: "Skylark 26 calling. Are you receiving me?" Ground Control should reply: "Receiving you loud and clear," etc. etc. You then state your message. It's all quite simple really. Have you got your map? Good. It's a nice day, so you'll find your way around without calling. Stay up for an hour or thereabouts. Remember that this first solo flight is classed as "Flight Experience"! So take it easy. Practice turns, climbing and generally getting used to the feel of it. Don't go higher than three thousand feet. You won't need oxygen, of course; that will come later. And for Christ's sake, keep an eye open for other aircraft: there'll be a lot of activity today. Two quick tips: you might find that the selection of the undercarriage lever is a bit tricky, so watch it; and when you've landed, go easy on the brake lever—gently does it!'

With that, Whitty left me to it and later I taxied slowly out onto the main grass area. I suddenly felt a mixture of excitement and intensity, a feeling I had never experienced in my life before. I thought, Why? I had no such feelings when flying solo on the Tiger Moth or the Harvard. Was it due to the famous legendary nature of this aircraft, the Hawker Hurricane? I recalled that Dowding had once stated that if you could fly a Hurricane, you could fly any single-engined fighter. I forced myself to keep calm as I finally stopped across wind, then completed the cockpit drill and other final checks. Control had already given me the all-clear for take-off. I clipped my face mask into place that housed R/T and oxygen supply (if required, that is). Flight path ahead across the grass: clear. No other aircraft taking off or landing. Throttle opened gently—aircraft surges forward; tail soon comes up, then airborne around the 90 mph mark. Some difficulty selecting the undercarriage lever to raise the wheels; a bit of a wobble as I did so, but then … sheer elation as the machine soared forward into a steady climb. Mixture lever eased back, propeller pitch next … to a coarser cut. Then a levelling out at 1,000 feet. Great! Great! Shouted to the world at large—if anyone was listening. I turned slowly to port to leave the circuit, straightened, then pulled the canopy back to look out below. The view was sheer magic. I was over the Wash, and stretching away to the East was the sweep of the sandy shores curving round along the Norfolk coastline. Speed now nearly 200 mph.

For the next hour or so, I cruised around getting the feel of it, but sticking to simple manoeuvres: medium turns, gentle climbing, checking the trim of the aircraft, and other pertinent exercises. Then, for the latter part of the flight, I concentrated on picking out landmarks, a vital undertaking for future safety.

I glanced at the time. I had been airborne for exactly one hour. It was time to land, so I turned towards the aerodrome. There were one or two aircraft in the vicinity by now, a couple of Hurricanes in the distance—could be Ward or Wills, I mused with a smile. Then the smile was withdrawn as I moved into the standard manoeuvres for the circuit and landing. This one was going to be the most exacting I had ever done, no question. Landing a Hurricane on grass ... phew!

I called in to Control. Message received: all clear for approach and landing. Down wind, undercarriage down, the drag slows the aircraft, speed about 150 mph, height about 1,000 feet. Then a gentle port turn to lose about 500 feet across wind some way past the edge of the 'drome. Now into wind to make a straight approach. Height now 500 feet and landing path dead ahead. Speed just over 100 mph. Trim checked and flaps lowered. From now on use of throttle linked to angle of glide. Now over the edge of the 'drome, throttle back, aircraft eased into standard landing. Down safely. Not quite a three-pointer, but good enough. Flaps up, taxying now towards the flight hut. I sighed; a deep, deep breath. My smile returned. I felt as if I had crossed some kind of barrier.

The three 'W's were stationed at Sutton Bridge for two months. During that time we went through the standard 'Sequence of Instructions' on type, plus one or two more flights in the Master. Halfway through the course, we were subjected to tests in a pressure chamber where we experienced what happened when deprived of oxygen. Not a nice experience.

Initially, night flying was limited. I clocked up only seven hours, mainly because no one expected day fighter pilots to do much night flying once they were posted to day-fighter squadrons. Most of the pilots were involved in the routine dispersal of the Hurricanes to nearby landing strips. It certainly disrupted our lives somewhat. The kites had to be collected at first light, and one night Jimmy Ward and I were on this very duty, so we had to have our names placed on the 'early call' register at the Guard House. At this aerodrome, like all others on the East Coast, lights of any kind were practically non-existent, and our dormitory—just a long wooden hut with beds on either side—only had blue lights fitted to the ceiling. My call was the first, at around five o'clock; Jimmy Ward's call was for an hour later. Unfortunately, the guard got it all wrong and instead of coming to me first, he went to Jimmy, who was fast asleep, shook him and said, "Are you Wild?" Jimmy jumped out of his skin and roared when he saw the time. "Wild! Wild! I'm bloody furious—b... off!"

Part way through the course, the CO called an urgent meeting of all flying personnel to inform them about an important announcement from

RAF Headquarters. Owing to the increased bombing missions by German aircraft on major cities at night, like London, Birmingham, Liverpool, Manchester and Belfast, new night-fighter Squadrons would have to be formed to combat this new menace. It really went to emphasise the fact that the Battle of Britain successes had prompted the enemy to alter their tactics to embark on the night bombing of Great Britain. Because of this, a night-fighter flight was going to be formed for training pilots for this special job. As a result of the eye tests we underwent while at Uxbridge, a dozen names were put up to form this flight, who could volunteer if they wished, and I was one of them; but not so Jimmy, Bernard and Dick. However, several of the original candidates climbed down and so my three friends stepped in. We were told that we would have to be interviewed later, and we were also informed that if we were accepted, we would be leaving Sutton Bridge within a few weeks.

The night-flying programme was stepped up, and for several days we were piling the hours in, both day and night. We did not do operational type of night work. We only did training with circuits and bumps (landing and taking off again immediately), and a few cross-countries navigated by linking up with beacons in various parts of East Anglia. Even so, although I only completed 7.35 hours in total, my baptism was the toughest possible. For one thing the Hurricane was not an ideal kite for flying at night with its poor cockpit visibility, and having to land the thing on grass was always tricky, but even more so in the dark. Also, because this aerodrome was on the East Coast, lights were at a minimum: no outer circle lights, no floodlight for take-off or landing, and only four Glim lamps for the flare path. From June 16th to 25th there was no moon. To add to the excitement, on the night of June 21st, I nearly 'bought it'. At the end of a 30-minute flight on a night with a lot of flying activity, my Hurricane was detailed to be 'stacked' over a beacon to wait for landing, each aircraft waiting its turn at a certain altitude. I was orbiting at 3,000 feet, with some aircraft above and some below. I had been waiting my turn and circling patiently for about five minutes when suddenly in the half-moonlight, a large dark mass of aeroplane suddenly flashed by at great speed and so close that I recognised it at once as a Wellington bomber. It took a while for my heart rate to get back to normal.

The next day, I was walking round the perimeter track in the sunshine with Jimmy Ward when we had a surprising and interesting encounter. We stopped in our stride as we noticed a Gloster Gladiator single-seater biplane, coming in to land. This was a pre-war fighter, and probably the most famous aircraft of its day. We knew that some of these planes were sent to Malta early in the war to defend the island from aerial attacks. The two of us watched the landing; hardly moving a muscle, we were so stunned by its presence. The landing was perfect. It seemed to float for ages before touch-down; so slow compared to a Hurricane's landing speed. Then, surprisingly, instead of taxying to the Control Tower as we would have expected, it headed slowly for the 'A' Flight complex. We started to run in that direction, eager to be there as the pilot emerged from the cockpit. 'I say,' said Jimmy, panting a little, 'With a bit of luck, whoever's flying it might let us have a browse round it. Or even let us sit in the cockpit.' Slightly out of breath, we arrived just before the engine was switched off, and we watched with interest as the pilot looked towards us. We noticed a fur collar close to the neck as he took off his flying helmet. Then he bent his head forward and down as he looked for something below. A moment later, an officer's peaked hat was placed on his head, and a few seconds later the pilot was standing a few yards from us on the tarmac. We were awestruck when we noticed a large amount of 'scrambled egg' on the peak. And then the shock: it was Air Chief Marshal Lord Dowding, who had dropped in to see his son. We decided to call it a day.

The course ended on June 25th and after a successful interview and medical at Uxbridge Reception Camp, the three 'W's and two others said goodbye to Sutton Bridge and our colleagues still on the course. We were given a very welcome seven days home leave before being posted to Valley, in Anglesey, where a new Australian night-fighter squadron, 456, was going to be formed, mainly staffed with Australians and with just a few English pilots and gunners.

4

Defiant Night Flights

The Germans' occupation of northern France enabled them better to attack Britain's north western cities, docks and factories, though London as ever took the brunt of the bombing. The Blitz continued to rage into 1941 and Liverpool suffered badly, particularly in the eight consecutive raids in May in which 1,450 died and over a thousand were seriously injured; 76,000 people were made homeless, the docks were badly damaged and 33 ships were sunk or destroyed. Similarly, large areas of Manchester were attacked and laid waste; and Belfast suffered the greatest loss of life in one night raid outside London when on Easter Tuesday, 15th April, 900 were killed and 1,500 injured, and almost half the houses in the city were destroyed or damaged. 456 Squadron, the Royal Australian Air Force's only dedicated night-fighter Squadron in the second world war, was part of the response in this region under the aegis of 9 Group RAF Fighter Command. Under the BCATP agreement, dedicated squadrons were formed for Commonwealth airmen trained within the scheme, enabling each government to retain some control and influence on the deployment of their air personnel. Most of this Squadron's crew would be Australian. For the Three W's, however, this particular fight was, literally, close to home.

Radar coverage was non-existent over Merseyside at the start of the war. Its installation along these coastal areas, and the development of inboard radar in the newer Beaufighters, was a critical development at this stage of the fight. Ground-Controlled Interception (GCI) radar became operational in May 1941, with all-round scanning capability; though it still had a long way to go to become fully effective.

July 1941. 456 (Australian) Squadron, Valley, Anglesey, North Wales

On July 10th 1941, with Jimmy Ward on the pillion of the good old motorbike, I reported to RAF Valley, near Holyhead on the coast of

Anglesey, where the single-engined aircraft in residence was the Boulton Paul Defiant. This aeroplane had received its baptism earlier in day fighting over the English Channel, when it took the Luftwaffe by surprise as a rear-guard fighter with the terrific fire power of four Browning machine guns in its gun turret. But once the Germans had gauged the limitations of its presence with Spitfires and Hurricanes, its efficacy declined. Because of the positioning of its guns, the Defiant could not engage the enemy dead ahead or from above, and in daytime it was vulnerable to the nose gunners of German bombers. Many had been shot down in head-on attacks. Now, at a critical time in night-fighting strategy, the Defiant, newly-painted black, was introduced into the fray. At this time, 1941 to 1942, it must be said that there was no such thing as a custom-built night-fighter aircraft: this was the only dedicated night-fighter we had at the time.

As the two of us entered the main gate, we realised immediately that this brand-new aerodrome with its hastily erected buildings was situated literally on the coast. The triangular form made by the runways criss-crossed the sand dunes. The usual Nissen huts of simple brick construction looked austere and, as we discovered later, so was the food and living accommodation. But it was midsummer and the weather was fine and warm. The island was completely flat, but we were quick to notice that south and south-east were the Welsh mountains and the awesome Snowdonia range. Ward actually gulped at the sight of them: there was no doubt they were a hazard that would have to be given the greatest respect.

We had already been informed that 456 Squadron was a brand new Australian night-fighter unit; so new, in fact, as we soon discovered, that they had no Aussie gunners to man the Defiants. Also, there were only a few pilots from 'down under', so several British aircrew were drafted in until the troop ship arrived in England. Bernard Wills had already arrived. We met him later.

It was nearing midday as we were directed to the CO's office, tucked away in the brick building in the centre of the complex. We received a friendly welcome from the Australian, a Sqn Ldr Olive DFC, a sturdily built man dressed in dark blue battle dress. He was dark haired, bronzed and around thirty years old. Once we were seated he addressed us in a typically strong Australian accent. 'I'm damned glad you've arrived as scheduled. We've had nothing but the gremlins at work in trying to get this outfit on an operational footing. I think you'll know that the ship bringing over our gunners has been delayed in transit. It'll be several weeks before they land here. We're even short of pilots. We have ten, that's all. The correct complement should be twenty or so.' He sighed. 'There are four gunners here, however: pommies.' He grinned. 'They've been lent to us. You'll have to share these blokes for a while as you gain experience on type, but the fact remains that you will also have to make several flights on your own until the gunners turn up, which will help you to become familiar with the kite's habits. Your Flight Commander will sort out which exercises to do.' He glanced down at some papers. 'Your gear has come. It arrived some days ago. I should settle in today, get used to the general layout of the place and its facilities. See my Adjutant; he's next door. He'll tell you where things are; sleeping quarters, Sergeant's Mess, etc.' He glanced at his watch and stood up. 'You'll be in 'A' Flight. Your Flight Commander is Flt Lt Hamilton. Report to him at nine tomorrow. He'll show you round the Defiant. And we're so keen to get you in the air, it's more than possible you might be able to fly one solo.' He paused as he reached the exit. 'Just a few words of advice. We are here to defend cities like Liverpool, Manchester and Belfast from night attack. This aerodrome is well placed for that, but it has some drawbacks when it comes to take-off and landing, particularly at night. The island is square-ish in shape, see? Well, you've got sea on three sides and mountains on the other, and there are sand dunes everywhere else; so you've not got much leeway. Make jolly sure you don't wander off the runways.' He suddenly grinned. 'But be like me—I'm an optimist!'

We spent the rest of the day, as instructed, settling in. That evening, in the Sergeant's Mess, we met the other sergeant pilots and sergeant gunners; all RAF crews apart from five Australian pilots. We soon mixed, and, as the bar was flung open for beer consumption, the room was alive with the sound of friendly chatter. At one stage, one of the Australians showed his skill on the piano to start a round of popular and sometimes bawdy songs. The three of us finally retired to the dormitory feeling slightly tipsy but all acknowledging that the evening had been a wonderful experience, and we happily voted Australia as one of our favourite countries.

At nine the following morning we were driven round to 'A' flight dispersal hut in the usual three-ton truck. There were six airmen aboard: four pilots, two gunners; all British. Apparently, Flt Lt Hamilton had driven there in his own car. As the truck slowly made its way round the perimeter track, we lapped up the glorious scenery of the mountains and the shore line, and were amazed at the extent of the sand dunes. As usual, there were two Flights, 'A' and 'B', and as we approached these huts, we only had eyes for the black-painted Defiants. I counted a dozen or so.

Once inside the flight building, we met our English Flight Commander, Ft Lt Hamilton, a young and rather dour individual who quickly drew our attention to the facilities, or lack of them, of the dispersal units. In a matter of minutes, we were led to a Defiant parked nearby.

Once again, on seeing a new plane for the first time in close up, I was surprised how large it looked. In actual fact it was only three feet or so longer than the Hurricane, but the presence of the dorsal gun turret, with its four Browning machine guns, situated directly behind the pilot's cockpit, gave the central fuselage a stocky appearance. It was powered by a Rolls Royce Merlin engine. To my eye, the fact that it was painted black made it look quite sinister.

Hamilton leaned against the trailing edge of the port wing where it joined the fuselage, took off his forage cap and stuffed it into the back pocket of his trousers, revealing a head of fair hair cut quite short. He mopped his brow. The others, too, could sense that it was going to be a hot day, and one or two jacket buttons were undone. Hamilton said, without a smile, 'You'll be pleased to know, I'm sure, that you—the pilots only—will be going solo this afternoon.' That brought grins to the faces of the four pilots. The two gunners knew that they would not be joining them until the pilots had gained some experience on type. He went on, 'Right, let me give you a brief outline of this aircraft before we climb up to look inside. No facts and figures: you'll be given pilot's notes when we return to the hut. This is just a natter about what this kite can or can't do. It's nice to fly even though it's heavier than other fighters. That's because of the turret, of course. You should have no difficulty with take-off or landing. However, it does have a tendency to swing to port on take-off as it gathers speed. Be aware of it. You'll soon adjust.' He directed his gaze towards the two English Gunners, Sgts House and Walker. 'You'll need to study the pilots' notes as well where clear instructions are laid down about the gun turret's handling.' Then we all walked slowly round the plane whilst he explained details.

Shortly after this preliminary talk, we were allowed to sit in the cockpits and gun turrets to 'browse', as Hamilton put it. About an hour later we returned to the hut where we had tea and coffee. Whilst we sat around and talked, we were issued with Pilot's Notes. These were ringed binders in orange-coloured covers. He said, 'I suggest you finish off the morning going back to the cockpit with this booklet in your hands and follow it closely as you look at the controls and instruments. This afternoon, you four pilots be here at two sharp when you'll meet three other Aussies, colleagues of mine, who'll give you a final cockpit drill before you go solo.'

After our second visit to the Defiant, we walked back to the Sergeants' Mess for lunch. Afterwards, over cups of coffee, the three of us were having a moan about the fact that since joining the RAF about a year previously, we still had not a single operational flight to our credit to enter in our logbooks, and it seemed certain that for some time yet we would be flying 'peaceful' hours while we gained air experience on the Defiant, plus the fact that this squadron was not yet on an operational footing because of the absence of the main batch of gunners. We then crossed the campus to gather our flying gear from the dormitory. Later we would place it in lockers at the flight hut. At 2 p.m. sharp we reported to 'A' Flight. By 2.15, I was seated in Defiant No. AA47, and Flt Lt Hamilton was standing on the wing beside me checking over the cockpit drill. After checking parachute and harness, Hamilton was saying, 'OK, Bryan, read aloud to me your cockpit drill. I'm sure you'll find it easy. Just say what you're going to say when you get to the end of the runway. Let's have it then.' For the next few minutes I went over the drill. Hamilton was completely satisfied: I had got it pat. 'It's all yours: go to it!' he said with a huge grin. 'You should stay up for about an hour getting used to the feel of it. Also, because it's a perfect day, suss out the Snowdon range and the Caernarvon Peninsula. Look out for Penrhos aerodrome near Pwllheli on the south coast; it's useful to know where that is: there are not many other places to land if some emergency crops up. One final thing: no more take-offs and landings after this solo: you'll be spending several hours later just doing circuits and bumps. Don't forget to call control.'

A short time later, I taxied slowly away from dispersal onto the perimeter track (without a gunner). Control had given the all-clear. I was aware that in other parts of the aerodrome, other pilots were going through the same drill, but I was the first away.

After the imperative cockpit drill at the end of the runway, I executed a perfect take-off, making sure I allowed for the slight swing to port. There was no difficulty. Wheels up around 90 mph, a rapid climb to level off at 1,000 feet over the sea. Then a slow, climbing turn towards the land to level off once more at 2,000 feet to settle into a steady cruising speed of 150 mph. I had noted this in the pilot's notes as the recommended speed for general level flying. For an hour or so I cruised round the whole area of the North Wales coast. Over the land I was forced to climb to over 3,000 feet to give myself plenty of clearance. The beauty of the area left me breathless—such a contrast with the flatness of the East Coast. I was particularly impressed by the Menai Straits, with its two bridges linking the island with the mainland. My landing was not quite perfect, but acceptable enough to complete a successful solo.

That evening some of the officers were in the Mess as guests and there was much celebrating because all the pilots had gone solo on type. We all agreed that the Defiant was a nice kite to fly. Apparently no one had come across any snags. During the course of the evening, it came to light that there had been some enemy activity in the region. Ground Radar Stations had plotted several enemy in the Irish sea. It was suggested that mine laying to destroy our shipping was probably the object of the intruders.

The buffet was in full swing when Flt Lt Hamilton was prompted by a question from Bernard Wills to outline briefly the Defiant's method of attack. The first unit to come into the equation was the Ground Control Radar Station for the region (GCI—the 'I' was for Interception). The controller would direct the fighter to the area where an interception might—only might—be made. If the fighter was lucky enough to be able to turn behind the bandit (code word for enemy aircraft), then had the power to catch him up, he might—only might—be lucky enough to pick him out of the night sky—using his eyes, of course: there was no radar housed in the Defiant. Only then would the pilot be able to edge underneath the belly of the intruder to enable the gunner to fire a devastating blast of gunfire upwards into the heart of the German plane. We listened with intense interest to this account, and we wondered how long it would be before we, too, would be carrying this out in practice.

For the next few weeks, we flew the Defiant, without a gunner on most occasions, clocking up the day hours of aircraft experience, and making entries in our log books with such titles as: 'circuits and landings', 'local cloud and instrument flying', 'Ground Control Interception test', 'homings up to 50 miles', 'combat practice', etc. There was an early casualty. 25-year-old Sgt Alan Brookes was killed on July 21st while low-flying over the island. This was particularly tragic as he was married. He was buried in Holyhead.

I found the Defiant a lovely machine to fly, and I liked it right from the start. It was especially good on instrument flying. But it was slow. Even at this early stage we realised that the chances of shooting down an enemy bomber were remote.

Not until three weeks after the solo did the two English gunners, Fred House and Teddy Walker, start to fly with the new pilots. Fred House was an experienced gunner, mainly on Sunderlands. He was Flt Lt Hamilton's gunner, while Walker was teamed with Flt Sgt Harry Dodson. Teddy Walker flew with me once or twice, and was with me on July 26th when I had my accident. It was only on our second trip together that disaster struck. The resulting crash was so horrific that the CO could not believe that the two occupants could ever survive. To make matters worse, it happened at night: only my second night flight in the Defiant.

The day before we had carried out a Night Flying Test (NFT) lasting one hour, followed by my first ever night flight in a Defiant. No problems with this: a fine night, half moon, airborne for one hour. The very next night we were airborne on a flight scheduled for one hour approximately, again with very good visibility. The exercise was dubbed as 'Homings up to 50 miles'. Coming back towards base, I called Control for permission to land. The all-clear was given and from the direction of the mainland, I started my approach to head westward; in other words, heading towards the sea. It was a clear night. The runway lights were on; the main floodlight to the left of the runway was lighting up the runway itself.

Everything was correct for the coming landing. Undercarriage was down; green light in the cockpit confirmed this. Distance from the flare path now about two miles; height 500 feet. Flaps now lowered, speed 140 mph. At this point I asked Walker on the intercom if everything was in order: answer affirmative. In a few minutes, about a mile to go, the height had dropped gently to 200 feet and speed also reduced to 130 mph. Here, I could clearly see one of the coloured lights beaming towards me from the Glide Path Indicator. This was situated at the side of the runway and was a simple but very clever gadget in the form of a large metal box that had a strong light inside it beaming up to the oncoming aircraft. It showed the pilot one of three colours depending on how the aircraft was approaching according to the angle of the aircraft in relation to the runway. If the aircraft was too high, he saw yellow, warning him to throttle back to prevent him overshooting. If the aircraft was too low, he saw red, warning him to use more engine power to enable him to reach the landing strip. If his angle of approach was just right, he saw green. This helped the pilot to manoeuvre the aircraft into the correct gliding angle for the landing. At night, a gliding or engine-assisted approach was more difficult to judge, so this indicator was invaluable. If one was to analyse a number of night landings, the green light would only be showing for perhaps half of them. On this particular night, as chance would have it, I had locked myself into the correct approach. That fact was to save our lives.

The Defiant was now coming over the edge of the aerodrome at 110 mph, height above ground about 12 feet or so. Everything seemed straightforward for the touchdown. And then, out of the blue—or rather the darkness—there was a terrific bang. At the same time there was a slight shudder from the aircraft. I shouted to my gunner: 'God! We've bloody well hit something!"

Of course, we had no idea what had happened, but the 'something' was a 12-foot high cookhouse trailer, being towed by a tractor round the perimeter track to one of the dispersal huts to provide instant meals for the ground crews on night duty. The driver and the cook were both on the tractor—fortunately for them. The aerodrome control pilot at the floodlight flashed the usual red light to tell the driver to halt, but for some unknown reason, he ignored it. He crossed the end of the runway as I entered the flight path zone. The starboard oleo leg on the Defiant had hit the top front corner of the trailer, and it had snapped off at the top of the leg to bury itself inside the van, smashing it to pieces.

To my immediate astonishment, the aircraft was still descending to the runway on an even keel. My mind worked at lightning speed in deciding to land the plane come what may. I couldn't risk opening the throttle to go round again. Had the propeller been struck? Was the undercarriage still

intact? Had a wing been damaged? And there was always the black sea
out front: I didn't fancy the idea of landing in that, which would happen if
the engine didn't respond. Also, words of wisdom from the CO flashed in
my mind, 'Don't wander off the runway because of the sand dunes.' I had
no time to call Control.

The Defiant was about to touchdown. The floodlight flashed by. What
about the wheels—were they still there? A screech of a tyre; the plane
held its course—no, no, something was not quite right. Ye gods! I knew
at once that the starboard wing was beginning to dip. I slapped the spade
grip control column to port—the wing steadied. I realised in a flash that
I was about to execute a one wheel landing. I shouted this fact to Walker.
How long could I hold it level? I had to throttle back: the runway wasn't
endless! Canopy opened.

Suddenly the starboard wing started to dip again. I throttled right back
and switched off the engine; mags off. Then one hell of a scraping noise
as the wing tip touched the runway—followed by an even more terrifying
cacophony of sound as the port wheel folded and the oleo leg shot upwards
into the body of the wing. The aircraft spun on its belly to starboard, shot
off the runway and came to an immediate stop, buried in a sand dune.

Complete silence. Teddy Walker was already scrambling out of the
turret and helped me to get unstrapped. Then there was a hissing noise
from somewhere and a smell of petrol fume. But thankfully, no fire; the
sand must have killed off the resultant sparks. We ran from the wreckage,
though, just in case, as fast as we could, and at that moment we heard in
the distance the alarm bells ringing from approaching vehicles, fire wagons
and ambulances. At a safe distance, we stopped to look back. Apart from
the torn wing surface where the undercart had penetrated, the Defiant
seemed to be nestling peacefully in the sand. The whole incident, from the
moment of impact, had taken about five minutes.

Somewhat shaken, we were taken to the Medical Room where the
Squadron doctor, in the presence of the CO Sqn Ldr Olive and the Flight
Commander Flt Lt Hamilton, eventually pronounced us 'reasonably OK
under the circumstances.' It was then that Flt Lt Hamilton told us the full
details about the trailer and that there would be an immediate inquiry. He
also praised me for the way in which I had handled the situation, and then
listened to my brief account of the incident.

Then Sqn Ldr Olive made an interesting assessment as to what might
have happened if the aircraft had been on either the yellow approach
or the red approach. It made my flesh creep as he explained, 'If you had
slotted onto the yellow glide angle, I think the wheel only would have hit
the trailer roof. In that case, I'm sure the nose would have been forced
down and the plane would have nosedived straight into the deck.' Walker

and I both shuddered. 'But even worse than that, if you had been on the red light, undershooting in other words, you would have increased speed and hit the trailer head on.' He suddenly clapped his hands together. No further words were needed. I gulped. The CO smiled. 'A strange way to go into the cookhouse for a meal'. I believe that the cook and his assistant were court martialled out of the RAF.

When the officers were convinced that we were not too shocked, they suggested that an early night, with a couple of aspirins, might be in order. But we were not allowed to retire early as the rest of the aircrew demanded our presence in the Sergeant's Mess for a complete talk-through of the incident over pints of beer and glasses of scotch. The verdict was that we were the luckiest men in the world that night to be alive.

For the next few weeks, with no gunners in sight apart from the four English airmen, I was clocking up the day and night hours with all kinds of exercises. Four out of five trips were without a gunner. The average time in the air worked out at about one hour fifteen minutes. The two Flights, 'A' and 'B', shared the same hut, each group flying two days on and two days off. This routine was to be the pattern of duty throughout my flying career as a night fighter pilot.

During this time I managed to drive home to Bolton on my motorcycle on a 48-hour pass. And on certain other days, I and a few of my colleagues were able to wander into Bangor or even Llandudno. There seemed to be no shortage of beer in the pubs, but there certainly was a shortage of food, and we often returned to camp hungry.

At last, at the beginning of August, the Aussie gunners arrived, about a dozen or so. The very next day, they and the whole squadron aircrew assembled in the Sergeant's Mess. They were all sergeants apart from one, a Pilot Officer, their leader throughout the journey from Australia. I also noticed that they were all on the small side. I thought, 'They'll have no trouble fitting into the turrets!' The main reason for this gathering was to get the pilots teamed up. Jimmy and I were interested to see how it was going to be carried out. The CO soon gave the clue. 'Right. It's now eleven o'clock. I've given permission for your bar to be opened. Let's get a few drinks in circulation and I suggest you simply get to know each other, and then I hope you'll mutually agree—pilot and gunner—to team up. I can't think of any other way of doing it. We haven't got bloody time to mess about in any case. I need to have you lot on an operation footing damn quick. So: the bar's open and the drinks are on me.' That raised a cheer, and someone called out cheekily, 'Good on you!'

For the next half hour or so we milled about and chatted endlessly. Some early pairings edged away to take seats to talk details, including Ward and Wills, and I suddenly felt uneasy at not having made a 'choice'. And then the dilemma was solved in a surprising fashion. A gunner came up to me as I was just leaving the bar with a pint of ale. Like all the Aussies, he was dressed in dark blue battle dress with the gunners badge with a single wing, on his left breast. At six foot tall myself, I found myself looking down on this man who seemed to be the smallest man in the room. He also may have been the oldest, I thought. His face was lined, hair ginger-ish, tough looking, stocky and very well-built, but as I had noticed earlier when I had had a few words with him, there seemed to be a gentle smile pinned to his face. The eyes, too, were a smiling blue. I was taken by surprise when the gunner stood right in front of me, and, bypassing the pint glass, tapped me on the chest with a forefinger and said, 'Have you teamed up with anyone yet?'

I grinned. 'No'

'How about having me, then, cobber?'

For a moment this caught me wrong-footed. I paused and then cursed myself for being so insensitive. 'Well, er ... yes ... yes ... O.K. I'm Bryan Wild. Pleased to meet you.' We shook hands. The hand was strong and the grip surprisingly firm.

'I'm Stan Greenwood.'

We sat down at one of the tables. I went to the bar and ordered a scotch for my new crewman. We talked for some considerable time about the main points of our lives. He came from Perth, Western Australia, and was unmarried. Out of sheer politeness I refrained from asking his age, but surmised that he was in his early thirties. He was nicknamed 'Ack'.

A little while later, when Ack had left the room, Sqn Ldr Olive walked over to my table and took a seat. 'I see you've teamed up with Ack Greenwood,' he said. 'You ought to consider yourself fortunate. He's the only gunner in this outfit classed as "Exceptional". If you're ever lucky enough to get close to an enemy aircraft he won't miss when shooting at it. I can also tell you that he used to be a champion boxer, a bantamweight; he's as tough as nails. And one other thing: watch out when you shake hands with him!' He smiled and left.

From that day the new pairing of Wild and Greenwood settled down to the serious business of gaining experience on type; not only the experience of flying the Defiant, but getting to grips with the technique of aerial interception and combat manoeuvres. This of course meant complete understanding of the contact with Ground Control Interception network. We were now beginning to clock up more night flying hours than day work. When any night flight was scheduled, the aircraft was always tested beforehand during the day in the Night Flying Test (NFT). This type of sortie would probably last no longer than 30 minutes. Patrols and other operational flights at night usually averaged out at 1.50.

During this spell of intense training, we became firm friends. I found my partner to be a most likeable and popular character, full of fun; altogether a lovely man. I was still very young, now approaching my twentieth birthday, and in many ways Ack was a fatherly figure to me. Outside of flying hours we continued to have a good time away from the aerodrome. On one occasion Ack and I flew to the Isle of Man just to land there and return, but the batteries went for a burton so we went into Ramsey while they were being fixed, and nearly bought the town up. We got bacon, tea, sugar and lots of other goodies. We flew home just after dark, with Ack carrying all the stuff on his knees in the turret. I sent a parcel of the goods home, and did they appreciate it! On a number of occasions, Jimmy Ward and I, with our new gunners, flew together to Penrhos to see a friend of ours. At the same time I still had the motor bike so it enabled me to travel about on nights off with either Ack or Jimmy to places the other chaps couldn't reach, especially to towns on the North Wales coast like Bangor (22 miles) or Llandudno (50 miles). We steered clear of Holyhead. Quite by accident we found a small café in Valley, really no more than a terraced house, where the lady cooked home-cured ham and eggs—what luxury! At last we had enough to eat. We kept it a secret for months. On October 8th 1941, the Army anti-aircraft training school at Rhosneigr nearby invited twelve of us to their ATS dance, so Jimmy and I went along together with ten gunners, including Ack. Apart from Ack collecting the officer's 'pips' and pinching the guitar from the band, everything went very smoothly. The following day, Teddy Walker, Fred House and I hitch-hiked into Llandudno, and met a Mrs Clarke, who offered to put us up for the night if we wished to stay. It turned out she owned a boarding house full of Civil Service girls to whom we were later introduced. They proved to be a very nice bunch. Every time we visited Llandudno we stopped with Mrs Clarke, who kindly gave us a room on the top floor. On one of the nights out when Ack was with us, he got a little merry and hit a 6′ 2″ policeman, who gently hit him back and laid him cold. Ack found himself in jail, but was released next morning for a fine of ten shillings. He didn't seem a bit worried.

I had my first operational scramble on September 4th but Sgt Fred House was with me instead of Ack Greenwood. We were off in three minutes from the phone call on a night scramble. We were told that a 'Hun' was mine-laying off Holyhead. It was half-moon, but there was a thick haze to 5,000 feet, and although we searched high and low, we go no visual. Better luck next time, I thought. On Sept 17th I went home by motorbike on a few days leave and on my return I had another night scramble, this time with Ack, but once more the Hun disappeared. In the meantime, I flew nearly every night and the hours were beginning to pile on.

We now settled into the standard night duty routine of the 'state of readiness' at the dispersal hut from dusk until dawn. There were usually six aircraft available for the night shift, so six crews were placed on standby and numbered one to six. Number 1 crew, pilot and gunner, would be the first to be scrambled if a call came through from Control for a possible interception or patrol mission. Number 2 crew would then be moved up to position Number 1, and so on. On a night when there was a great deal of activity, it was quite possible for Number 1, after returning to base and being placed at the bottom of the list, to be scrambled again, thus involving them in two sorties for that night. This Flight group of six crews would be on duty for two successive nights, then have two nights off.

It soon became clear to Ack Greenwood and I that we were carrying out more patrols than actually being scrambled to meet enemy aircraft. Indeed, as years went by, I would find that the majority of my flying hours were allocated to soulless patrols. Most of these were carried out over the sea, their purpose being, so I surmised, a kind of deterrent, and it was obviously an advantage to have an attacking aircraft already airborne and at a useful altitude in case an enemy plane was about to wing its way towards Great Britain.

These pilots and gunners, of course, had to be present at the dispersal throughout the night, so there was a dormitory at the rear of the hut where the crews at the bottom of the list could sleep if they wanted. In many cases there were no calls for a scramble, in which case they had a good night's rest. However, on a busy night, the din was not very conducive to sleep: telephones ringing, clattering feet as airmen dashed about the wooden floors, engines being started, etc. On a night when enemy activity was plotted on the radar screens, the crews, quite naturally, were somewhat tensed up. When the first scrambles had been called, those crews lower down the list were immediately alerted, so sleep for that night was impossible. And if this situation occurred for two nights in succession, the pilots and gunners found themselves completely tired out the next day, and usually slept through the whole morning and afternoon. These airmen took a pride in getting airborne in the shortest possible time. There were several ploys to keep the scramble efficient. The parachute was always placed beforehand in the bucket seat of the aircraft. The gunner's parachute was in 'pack' form to be attached to a harness at chest position, so he carried his out to the aircraft. Readiness pilots were dressed ready to go, complete with a Mae West life jacket. The aircraft was always positioned for easy take-off.

During the months of October 1941, I was only involved in four operational sorties; three were night patrols over the Irish Sea, and one was a scramble against a low flying enemy aircraft off the Welsh Coast, possibly laying sea mines. As with so many other sorties, this flight proved frustrating, because although Control directed us to the area with radar contact and said that the Defiant was very close to it, we saw nothing because of patchy fog in the region.

In this same month, I was involved in three separate dangerous incidents; two at night, the other during daytime. This daylight incident materialised unexpectedly on a very cloudy day when we were well above cloud at about 10,000 feet. We had just completed a height test at 20,000 feet when we decided to return to base. I knew that I would have to get a radio fix to descend safely away from the Snowdonia range, because the cloud base had been as low as 500 feet on take off. A fix was a message from Control to the pilot stating the exact position map-wise of the aircraft. The drill for this was quite straightforward. The pilot would make repeated short radio transmissions every minute or so which were picked up by three ground radio stations. Some bizarre things were heard in the control room on these occasions. The usual thing would be a nursery rhyme but sometimes there were more lurid transmissions. Each station would each receive this 'bearing line' and Control would immediately note the intersection of the three lines to gain a cross-fix of the plane's exact position. The map reference would then be transmitted back to the pilot as soon as possible. Sometimes the pilot needed to make quite a few transmissions to plot the course.

On this occasion, to my dismay, there was no reply to my nursery rhymes and I realised immediately that the RT had packed up. I then talked the dilemma over with Ack, both of us trying to guess whereabouts over Wales we were. We had been flying for nearly two hours and fuel consumption had to be a major factor in the coming flight plan. I felt a slight churning in my stomach. There was only one way to tackle it. First, to guess our position in relation to the ground. Then I would have to descend gradually through cloud on a westerly course that would take us out to the Irish Sea. If I went too far west I could find myself so far out that I would not have enough fuel to reach base. I glanced at the fuel gauge again. It was running low.

So, staying on the same course, I soon levelled off at 5,000 feet, just above cloud tops. I checked my speed: 180 mph. I would travel roughly three miles in one minute. I guessed we were somewhere over Cheshire. How many miles as the crow flies from Cheshire to Anglesey? About fifty miles give or take. So, at three miles a minute that would take 16 minutes or so. I carefully timed this leg, skimming just above the clouds. There was no sun, there were other stratus clouds way above. When the time was up, still going west, I started the descent, lowering the speed considerably. In the cloud mass, I carefully watched the altimeter as it slowly registered the drop in height: 4,000 feet, 3,000 feet, 500 feet. God! Still no sign of the sky or the ground. My mind suddenly pictured the mountains ... the mountains!

Then suddenly, at 450 feet, a slight break in the cloud and more light filtering through the grey mass. Another gap, a bigger one this time. And suddenly, below, a stretch of sea, sand, a town ... Llandudno! Phew! It was as though a ton weight had been lifted off my shoulders. A cheerful shout from Ack. 'Great work, Bryan. I've just given birth to twins!'

It was an easy flight to base where they all wondered where on earth we had got to.

The following night a second incident took place which was potentially just as dangerous to our well-being. We had just finished an hour's patrol on a fine night, when we were recalled to base. On the circuit at a 1,000 feet and on the usual downwind leg, I selected undercarriage down. The undercart (u/c) lever was a short cast-iron handle about six inches long. To lower the undercart, the lever was pulled down through a slot in the control box. Next to this lever, in another slot, was the lever which operated the flaps. So that these two couldn't be confused, a metal stud at the base of the u/c handle had to be pressed with the pilot's thumb before it would operate. On this occasion, however, when I pressed this stud and selected in the usual way, the lever did come down, but the undercarriage didn't! The handle had snapped off somewhere inside the slotted box. I was left holding this lever and feeling absolutely astonished and angry. The red light u/c indicator was still on. How the hell was I going to lower the undercart when there was no lever to grab hold of?

I told Ack what had happened and then carried on round the circuit while I told Control of the problem over the RT. Whist I was waiting for some words of wisdom from Control, I tried getting hold of the stud, the only part of the unit left clear of the slot. I tried to press it in order to move it down, but to no avail. Even when I donned a flying glove it still wouldn't budge. Angry, I snapped aloud, 'A hammer, a hammer, my kingdom for a bloody hammer!' thinking that a heavy blow on the stud with something substantial would do the trick. I couldn't think of any such object available in the cockpit.

I had visions of flying round for ages and eventually having to belly-land it on the runway, a tricky and dangerous thing to do at the best of times, but especially at night. Still no reply from control. They had obviously never come across such a strange mishap before. It's not every day that an undercarriage lever breaks off in a pilot's hand. And then, out of the blue, I thought of a possible solution. Would the heel of my leather flying boot fit the bill? Telling Ack of my intention and not to mind if the aircraft rocked somewhat whilst I took the boot off, I did just that, and holding it my left hand at the 'neck' I struck the stud with the heel part. No joy. Another blow, with more force this time, and to my great relief the stud suddenly shot downwards through the slot and the undercart came down: green light on! Ack cheered, I gasped ... and almost forgot to put my boot back on before landing. A night flight which was scheduled for forty minutes had taken one hour thirty.

The third incident, near the end of October 1941, also happened at night and was even more hair-raising than the previous mishap. We had taken off in poor weather conditions on a patrol mission, but after half an hour's flying, we were hastily recalled as the weather deteriorated. By the time we reached base the cloud had clamped down thick and very low, down to 200 feet or so. I was the only aircraft (Defiant) flying and ground control ordered me to come in on 'ZZ' approach. There was obviously a bit of concern about the tricky situation with those on the ground—and in the air, too!

All pilots had at some time or another carried out the ZZ approach routine on the Link Trainer, the standard flight simulator. It was a controlled descent through cloud, when conditions warranted what one could safely call 'an emergency landing'. Most pilots had practised this in actual flying conditions and providing they followed the right procedure it wasn't too difficult. It started with the cross-fixing routine, which was carried out when the plane was actually over the aerodrome. Once the controller had the cross-fix on the plane's exact position, he would give the pilot a course to fly away from the aerodrome.

The pilot by this time would be at circuit level and seeing to undercarriage and flaps as usual, speed also controlled. About two miles from base, he would be told to do a gentle descending turn to head for the runway, already lit with flares and floodlight. At this point, if all was well, the pilot should be coming out of cloud and seeing the runway dead ahead. The rest would be easy.

In our case, all was not well! Once at the aerodrome and maintaining a height of 2,000 feet we had started on our outward run away from the aerodrome which had been plotted and given to us by our controller. Remember that while I was flying the damn thing at about 150 mph in the direction of the Welsh mountains, I was transmitting every minute or so and in return receiving the controller's instructions ('reduce height to 1,000 feet, steer 220°' etc.). I was flying absolutely blind on instruments in dense cloud and waiting intently for the crucial order to do a gentle 180° descending turn ready for the inward approach at a point around two miles from base. All well and good, with a little concentration. But at around 800 feet and before I reached the point for the turn, the controller almost screamed that one of the radio stations had packed in and therefore he couldn't fix my position or plot my approach. Those Welsh mountains once more loomed very large in my mind. I would have to come in on a wing and a prayer.

The ten thousand dollar question leapt instantly to my mind: when should I execute the turn to starboard through 180° to ensure I was on a reciprocal course heading back to base? If I left it too late I would crash into Snowdon, and if I turned too soon I would be too high to land on the runway. Also, if that happened I would have to go round again, maybe into cloud once more, and be completely lost. I knew of all things that I mustn't panic. I knew that I was due to make the 180° turn to the right because another few miles ahead were the mountains, so by sheer instinct, and a few encouraging words from 'Ack' in the turret, I judged the time to start the turn and reduced height at the same time. 'Thank the Lord the island is very flat,' I thought.

We were at about two hundred feet when suddenly we had a stroke of unbelievable luck. A gap appeared in the cloud below and to my right. I could hardly believe my eyes. I immediately recognised the Menai Straits and the bridges I had admired previously: such distinctive and welcome landmarks! Ack spotted them as well and shouted to me. Without a moment's hesitation, I turned to starboard and dived for the gap like a hawk striking for a mouse. As I pulled out of the dive just below cloud level, I checked my height: it was 150 feet. I immediately called in to base to tell them where I was, turning round all the time towards the 90° compass direction which would head me for the runway some miles away in the pouring rain. To my huge relief, through the murk of the downpour I could see the welcoming lights of the flare path ahead. My flight commander, Flt Lt Hamilton, had already assessed my predicament and had ordered all hands to light emergency oil flares on either side of the runway and had set the floodlight to full blast. I could have cheered. I was now even lower, at about 100 feet up over the dark countryside with wheels and flaps down and the engine almost at full throttle. I eventually made a safe landing. Sighs of relief all round.

I felt that I was getting my fair share of the gremlins at Valley. By this time in my flying career, however, I had formulated some ideas of my own about how to handle difficult situations, a kind of philosophy ingrained into my soul based on the one single thought of survival in the air. I realised early in my training that crises were bound to occur, and if I was to overcome the problem, whatever form it took, there was absolutely no use in becoming panic-stricken. In other words I forced myself to keep calm even though inwardly I would be frightened. An emergency had to be tackled with some urgency but not panic 'methods'. My experience taught me that the dividing line between urgency and panic is a very narrow line indeed. Even urgent moves or urgent thinking can cloud the issue but panic can paralyse thought altogether. So I concluded that the form was to move and think urgently, but *never, never* panic.

Later that month, the Squadron was due to be equipped with Mark II Beaufighters: the Merlin engine version and painted black. Almost at once I was posted to South Cerney near Cirencester with a number of others on a week's course for conversion to twin-engined flying. The aircraft used was the Oxford, with Cheetah engines. We found the course fairly easy and we quickly learned how to handle the plane. I was soon back at Valley with a recording in log books of the Oxford times: 10 hours dual, 17 hours solo, plus a couple of night trips.

But the very next day I learned something which was a bit of a bombshell. Ack and I were to be posted to 256 Squadron, Squires Gate, Blackpool along with two other crews. Roy Hedderley was very pleased to be going, because his wife was at Blackpool. But I felt quite dashed; Jimmy Ward and Bernard Wills were not coming with me this time. This was the first posting since Cambridge that I was without one or other of them. I was going to miss Jimmy in particular, because he had been with me all the way. Furthermore, I was bitterly disappointed that I would not have the chance of flying the Beau. To all intents and purposes, this aircraft was the first custom-built night-fighter with its inbuilt radar system. Inbuilt radar! Also, someone had informed me that 256 Squadron was still using Defiants. No Beaus on the horizon there, apparently. There was one small silver lining. I managed to squeeze a 48-hour pass out of the deal because my new posting was only thirty miles from home. This time I managed to catch up with my other brother, Frank, an RAF electrician based at Cosford. It was a very welcome relief before plunging into the next phase of my RAF career.

In a way, though I didn't see it at the time, I was fortunate to be posted to Squires Gate, Blackpool. The Beaufighter II—the Merlin powered job which I was awaiting so eagerly at Valley—proved to be a disaster. Among other faults it had a terrific swing on take-off and there were several fatal accidents involving this mark. It was soon withdrawn from service.

5

Close to Home

256 Squadron had been operational over south-west England until March 1941, when it was moved north to bolster the defences of Merseyside. 307 Squadron, which it replaced, had experienced a high number of accidents with their Defiants, and 256 Squadron followed suit to some extent. Squires Gate airfield, on the coast at Blackpool, had been requisitioned in 1938 and later improved when a factory producing Wellington bombers was built on the site. One problem with the station was the sand that was continually blowing across the aerodrome, getting into the air intakes of the engines; a persistent problem and a serious hazard that may possibly have contributed to some, but by no means all, of the more serious incidents. 256 Squadron took part in the defence of Liverpool during its worst bombing in May 1941. On the night of 7/8 May, it flew a total of twenty sorties, with three enemy aircraft destroyed and three probables. This was out of a total 339 sorties and 21 aircraft destroyed by Fighter Command as a whole on that night, a tally that may have helped turn the balance in the north west. Following this action, the Squadron's Flt Lt Christopher Deanesly was awarded the DFC and his gunner, Sgt. Scott, the DFM.

November 1941, 256 Squadron, Squires Gate, Blackpool

Early in November 1941, Ack Greenwood and I started a new period of service at the large Squires Gate aerodrome, right on the south side of Blackpool, by the sea front. This squadron was to offer night cover to such cities as Liverpool, Manchester and Belfast. On arrival we were directed to the Sergeant's Mess. We were surprised and pleased to find that it was a large hotel commandeered for RAF only, the Fairhaven, on the sea front at Ansdell near St Annes on Sea. Officers were billeted in another hotel in Blackpool. We were shown to our comfortable bedrooms on the first floor, where we discovered we would share the space with two other sergeants, both likeable-looking chaps: Ray Jeffs, a New Zealander, and his gunner, Deryk Hollinrake, a Yorkshireman from farming country around Todmorden. Deryk and I quickly became very good friends. I understood that early in the war, in another unit, he had been posted to France. When the Germans invaded, he and his colleagues had to escape south through France, mostly on foot until they finally managed to get a boat in Marseilles to bring them back to Liverpool. He didn't talk about it much; he was a very self-effacing man, with a lovely quiet but lively sense of humour. All the rooms had their original fixtures and fittings, apart from the beds, and we all thought we had landed on our feet. It was a happy billet. In time our room became rightly known as 'The Madhouse' because we were always having friendly fights.

During that first evening we were introduced to many of the Sgt Pilots and gunners. There were times when I couldn't help feeling somewhat depressed when my thoughts strayed to the friends I had left behind at Valley. However, after an excellent meal we all gathered round the bar. There were Canadians, Australians and New Zealanders among the

The Sergeants' Mess, Fairhaven Hotel, Andsell, was a happy billet. Seated, L to R: Sgt (Air Gunner) 'Red' Squires, ?, Sgt (Pilot) Ray Jeffs RNZAF, Sgt (Air Gunner) Stanley 'Ack' Greenwood RAAF, Sgt (Pilot) Bryan Wild. Next row, 3rd from right: Sgt (Pilot) Dove, RCAF.

aircrew and the atmosphere was relaxed and friendly. I felt that at least the social side of things had started well.

The next day, after another fine meal, we set off to report to 'A' Flight dispersal at the aerodrome, where, at ten o'clock, we were detailed to meet their Flight Commander, Flt Lt Donovan Toone. The dozen or so aircrew were transported from the Hotel by a three-ton truck with canvas cover over the rear section. It was a dry but cold day, so we were all wearing our greatcoats. As my home town of Bolton was only thirty miles away, I knew Blackpool very well, but I hadn't been there for some years and was enjoying my return visit immensely, especially as I had never been to the airport before. As we approached the main gate, I couldn't help looking round to see the famous Pleasure Beach nearby and the imposing Blackpool Tower in the background.

We were checked at the gate by the guards and then the truck turned left onto the perimeter track winding its way round the airfield with its three main runways in triangular form. On the way, we could see several types of aircraft parked at the two large hangars on the north side facing the main road: a Stirling bomber, two Westland Lysanders, a Botha, a Spitfire, and a Wellington bomber. I would see quite a few 'Wimpeys' later, because at the rear of the flight huts was a Shadow factory making these aircraft. As the truck approached the flight buildings I noted that there were several bomb bays with Defiants sheltering inside, protected by sandbagged walls. I spotted the Squadron's code letters on the side of the black fuselage. The large, Roman-type letters were 'JT' followed on the other side of the roundel by the letter of the aircraft, e.g., 'T', painted in an unusual dull red colour. The flight hut came into view as the truck turned a right-angled bend on the perimeter. There were several other buildings nearby, some of brick. Apparently at one time this whole area had been part of a large farm. The truck stopped outside the wooden hut and we all piled out to find seats in the main room. Once again, the interior was much the same as all the other flight dispersals I had seen so far. I had already been informed that the usual two Flights would be on night duty, each one in session for two nights, then having two nights off. Six or so aircraft would be on call. The other two crews from Valley were in 'B' Flight.

Within a few minutes we were listening to the Flight Commander, Flt Lt Donovan Toone. He was very tall, fair-haired and sported a moustache, a striking and friendly figure. He was saying, 'I see you've met the bods from Valley … Welcome to 'A' Flight'. He addressed Ack and I. 'I suggest you have a recce round the 'drome later this morning. You won't be on duty tonight. Then, at 12 o'clock, the CO wants to meet you. He'll be in later. His office is across the yard just outside here.' He paused to find a seat and then announced, 'Now, here's why I've been asked to call you all together.

You'll be pleased to hear, I'm sure, that very soon the Squadron is going to be equipped with Beaufighters.' There was a spontaneous cheer from the pilots. 'They won't be the Mark II versions. As you will know, they've had some trouble with those. These will be the radial jobs, the Hercules engines, and, of course, they have A1 Mark IV radar.' He stopped at that point to take a seat near the stove.

I suddenly noticed that the gunners, including Ack, had not joined in the general euphoria. One or two even had grim faces. It quickly dawned on me why they were looking nonplussed. Radar operators (RO's)were required for Beaus, not gunners. Toone sensed their uncertainty and said, 'These planes are not due for a week or so, and if any of you gunners would like to take on a special course for RO's to enable you to switch jobs, you must let the CO know when the time comes.' He paused to see if that had eased their anxiety, then went on, 'You'll be aware, I think, that down south, and especially in the London blitz area, the Beaufighter squadrons have had dramatic successes. You've all heard of the exploits of Group Captain John Cunningham, of 604 Squadron. And by the way, it's worth mentioning here that his radar operator, Jimmy Rawnsley, was a gunner to start with. Well, when we get some of these kites, perhaps we can do something useful with them up here in the north. Now, there's a good reason why I'm telling you now about the imminent arrival of the Beaus, pilots please note. Before you go solo on this aircraft you will first receive dual instruction on our Oxford, and then on a Blenheim, two of which will be delivered here tomorrow.' Glances of pleasure all round from the pilots. 'You may be interested to learn that the A1 radar was first installed in Blenheims in the early night-fighting sorties, but it wasn't very efficient, and in any case, the Blenheim was too slow.' He stood up. 'That's about it for now. NFT's as usual this afternoon.'

Later, after a walk around the aerodrome, Ack and I crossed the yard at the side of the flight hut to a stone building. Here we mounted an exterior flight of wooden stairs to a room on the first floor which served as the CO's office. We knocked on the door, were called to enter, then we saluted as we faced Sqn Ldr Christopher Deanesley DFC, seated at his desk.

Deanesley was well known in RAF circles. He was a former Battle of Britain pilot, on Spitfires, and during that time he had been hit with return fire and shot down twice over the sea. He had been lucky to come out of those incidents alive, having been wounded on both occasions. Not only that, and what impressed us more, perhaps, because closer to home for us, was that his 'kills' of four enemy planes were achieved on Defiants in 256 Squadron in the Spring of 1941, with the partnership of his gunner. He was a very large man, and seemed to us both physically and by reputation a powerful figure. He talked to us for some time, asking all kinds of

Pilot Officer Don Toone of 256 Squadron, with men from 'A' Flight outside their dispersal hut with a cross cut from his He. III 'kill' of 8 May 1941, which crashed on the River Dee marshes at Bagillt. Don Toone centre, hatted. Behind Toone and left of him in the photograph, Bryan Wild in front of doorway, with Mae West jacket. Front row, left to right: two unknown airmen; 3rd, Sgt (A/G) B. C. Simmonds, RNZAF; then Sgt (Plt) known as 'Juddy' RAAF, Sgt Al Hughes, and Plt Off. Johnny Tweedale.

questions about our careers in the RAF. He ended the talk by informing us that the next day we would be on night duty. He shook hands as we left, and we felt that his was a warm welcome. At the end of that afternoon, I bounded up the stairs of our billet whistling. My immediate impressions of my new posting were good. I was with a grand bunch of fellows. From what I had picked up, the comradeship of the squadron was first class, with a great, friendly relationship between officers and Sgt pilots and gunners. The CO was a bit of a card, an imposing character, and Flt Lt Don Toone was one of the nicest chaps anyone could meet.

We also became very friendly with a pilot called Joe Berry. He had recently been through a difficult time. He and his gunner, Flt Sgt Edward 'Ted' Williams, had been flying just north of Blackpool when their Defiant developed engine problems and eventually lost power altogether. They had to bale out at just under 5,000 feet. Ted went first but the wind took him out over the Irish sea, whereas Joe came down safely on land north of the airfield. The lifeboats searched in the dark for five hours, but tragically, though they heard Ted shouting several times, they just could not find him.

His body was washed to shore the next morning. This all happened just before we arrived.

That evening, Ack and I were joined by Jeffs and Hollinrake in catching the train for the short journey to Blackpool. In that one evening, our 256 'veteran' guides introduced us to most of the favourite pubs, cafes and night spots. After a meal at what was to become my favourite eatery, the Stanley Café, we all piled into the Galleon Bar in the Winter Gardens, part of which was actually called '256 Squadron Bar', then later to the Palatine bar opposite the station, and finally the session ended at the Casino on the South Shore. By the time we had trudged back to the station to catch the train back to Ansdell, we were in a merry mood. I remembered that night for a long time. I had never experienced anything like it since I was in Civvy Street. Blackpool was a good place to be stationed and we knew we were lucky to have plenty of entertainment on hand.

The following morning was a nice one weather-wise, with plenty of blue sky and broken clouds. Ack and I were still shaking off our slight hangovers when we joined all the members of 'A' and 'B' Flights and climbed aboard the two trucks parked outside the Hotel. We were all eager to be at the aerodrome because it had been announced earlier that the two Blenheims were being delivered around ten o'clock. It was still cold, so again greatcoats were being worn. On the way into Blackpool we learned from a sage that the two aircraft had been transferred from a bomber group somewhere in southern England. As expected, the Flight hut was crowded with aircrew, the number being swollen by the presence of officers. We

Transport to Squires Gate aerodrome, 1942. From right to left: Bryan Wild 3rd from right, Ray Jeffs, Deryk Hollinrake, Fred House, ?, Ack Greenwood. Joe Berry is 3rd from left.

256 Squadron aircrew January 1942. Back row (left to right: Bryan Wild (Pilot), Sgt 'Jock' Carr (Gunner), 'Ack' Greenwood (Aussie, Gunner), Sgt Alan Hughes (Gunner). Front row: Ray Jeffs (NZ, Pilot), Sgt. Johnny Newall (Aussie, Pilot), Sgt. Dave Clarke (Aussie, Gunner).

In February 1942, Sgt Carr was a passenger in a car driven by Plt Off. Johnny Newall which collided with a taxying Defiant. Carr was killed outright. Johnny Newall was found to be at fault.

246 Squadron footballers head back home, Squires Gate 1942. Ack Greenwood at the back of the line; Joe Berry third from front, behind Ray Jeffs.

Bryan Wild, centre, with colleagues in Blackpool, 1942.

Bryan Wild, Ack Greenwood and Fred House on a Boulton Paul Defiant in early February 1942. Ack Greenwood was killed on 7th of that month with Plt Off. Olney in an air crash off Lytham. Fred House was killed on the night of 25th January later the same year in a Whitney bomber shot down over Hamburg.

didn't have long to wait. Shortly after ten the two Blenheims landed and taxied directly over to the Flight dispersal. As soon as the engines were switched off, we surged forward to surround the planes. We were all rather surprised when we realised that one of the civilian pilots from the delivery flight turned out to be a woman. She made a few hearts flutter when the young and rather attractive aviator took off her flying helmet, let her long hair flow down to her shoulders, then threw us all a winning smile before striding off to meet the CO—'the lucky blighter!', we thought.

Eventually, Ack and I took our turn to inspect the Blenheim, in the early days of wartime designed as a three-seater fighter-bomber with a crew of pilot, bomb aimer and gunner, and with two Bristol Mercury engines. These had been fitted with dual control to enable pilots to have instruction before flying the more powerful Beaufighter. It seemed very long; over forty feet, and the wing span was even longer; over fifty. They were camouflaged in the usual brown and green colours. For the next few weeks, however, I had to forget this aircraft because some of the regular members of the squadron had been chosen first to have dual instruction. Instead, I found myself in a hectic spell of night flying on Defiants, carrying out many training exercises, noted in my log book under such headings as: 'Searchlight Co-operative, 'RT Homings', ZZ Landings,' Air combat', etc. During this time I was only involved in two operational patrols. In neither case was I called upon to engage the enemy. I hoped to travel home for Christmas 1941, but it was not to be. Night flying training went on relentlessly.

In early February 1942, the month I was made Flight Sergeant, I was asked by Don Toone if I would like to have 'a week's rest'. Apparently, a certain No. 3 Delivery Flight, based at High Ercall, near Shrewsbury, was desperately short of their complement of civilian pilots to deliver a variety of aircraft to and from various aerodromes throughout Great Britain. These planes were usually machines which had been sent to a Maintenance Unit (MU) for a general service, very similar to a person taking his car to a local garage for repairs or servicing, and then having to collect it later. Toone asked me if I would like a ten-day break to join this outfit. I didn't hesitate, and on February 3rd 1942, I duly arrived at High Ercall aerodrome. I was soon introduced to the Commanding Officer, Flt Lt Saunders, who explained the drill: we pilots ferried machines all over the place and he would pick us up in the pre-war passenger plane, the Dominie.

My very first outing was on February 7th in a Spitfire 11B, a machine I had never flown before. This particular aircraft 'belonged' to the unit, used specifically to let pilots obtain their first solo on type, so that from then on they were qualified to ferry this plane. As was the case with my first flight in a Hurricane, there was no way I could receive dual instruction on the

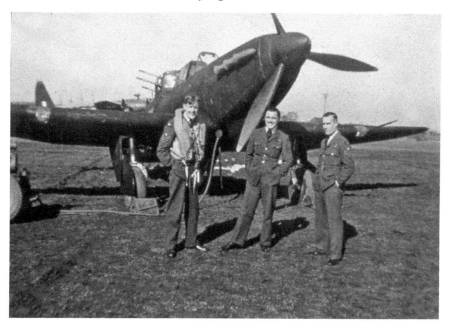

Bryan Wild (right) with ? and Fred House on left, in front of Defiant, 256 Sqn Squires Gate 1942.

Defiant JT-E in snow at Squires Gate—Bryan Wild and Ack Greenwood.

256 Squadron Christmas Dinner 1941.

From left to right: known airmen only:

Front row: 3rd Sgt (Pilot) Ray Jeffs, RNZAF, 5th Sgt (A/G) AI Hughes, Sgt. Bernard Simmonds RNZAF.

2nd row, 1st, Bryan Wild, 2nd Ack Greenwood, 4th Sgt (A/G) Fred House, 6th Sgt (A/G) Grimes, 7th Sgt Dove RCAF, 8th Sgt (A/G) Deryk Hollinrake.

3rd row, 1st (seated behind the table) Flt Sgt Chalmers, 3rd Sgt Morgan, 4th Plt Off. Oxlade (or Olney?), 6th Flt Lt Don Toone, 8th Flg Off. Harrison-Yates, 12th ?Sgt 'Titch' Barrett (seated at end of table).

4th row, 11th AC2 H. C. Skinner; just behind unknown 13th is Vogel.

Very back row of three on right: Bunny May, centre with his hands on the shoulders of Johnny Walker; 'Darky' Moore is immediately behind Walker. Robinson far right at back. *Names of airmen supplied by Russell Brown*

Defiant photographed over Squires Gate, Blackpool, in December 1941, flown by Pilot Sgt Ray Jeffs (NZ) with gunner W/O Deryk Hollinrake. Photograph taken from Defiant piloted by Bryan Wild with 'Ack' Greenwood, gunner.

Spitfire. Flt Lt Saunders stood on the wing and told me the gen about the controls and instruments, along with some advice on how to fly it. From then on it was up to me. I flew the Spitfire for about thirty minutes on local flying. I was amazed at the way it responded to the controls. It was a dream to fly. Like the Hurricane, I found the cockpit rather confined, and on landing I found the aircraft somewhat 'unwilling' to touch down; probably because I was going too fast.

The next day I was detailed to ferry Spitfire 11A down south to Llandow, South Wales. I would have to find my way there by map reading as there was no inboard RT connection. Like all pilots flying an aircraft like the Spitfire with a sliding canopy, I was wearing a flying helmet fitted with connection to RT and oxygen. As well as this, I always kept my flying goggles perched on the top of the helmet as an emergency. This ploy was mainly to protect my eyes in case of fire or an uncontrollable oil leak. The goggles' strap was threaded through a loop at the back of the helmet to keep it in place. It was because of these goggles that I was about to experience a nasty and rather bizarre incident. It was only the fact that I was a reasonable height above ground when it happened that saved me from disaster.

It was a fine day and, once airborne, I had no difficulty flying without a map most of the way. It was simply a case of following the River Severn

'My first flight in a Spitfire.' Spitfire GQ-S, High Ercall Delivery Flight, 7th February 1942.

to South Wales, the route easily seen through the clear cockpit canopy. When the coast came into view I turned to starboard to head towards the aerodrome at Llandow, not far from Bridgend. Nearing my destination and flying at 2,000 feet, I wanted to be sure of my position, so to get a clearer view of the ground I decided to pull back the sliding canopy and look out. To do this I released a metal catch at the front edge where it met the main windscreen and yanked backwards to pull the canopy over my head. As the hood shot back, this catch got entangled in the nose-bridge of the goggles, and my head was snapped back with tremendous force. I was locked there, with my gaze pinned upwards to the sky, unable to turn away. Within seconds, the Spitfire had thrown itself into a climbing, slow roll to starboard as the joystick was pulled involuntarily backwards. It then turned on its back and started to plunge to earth. I frantically wrestled with the helmet to tear it, literally, off my head. With seemingly superhuman effort I managed it eventually. Only then could I direct my attention to getting the aircraft back to normal flight. But by this time the altitude needle was throwing away hundreds of feet and as I eventually levelled out I was shocked to find that I was down to less than 500 feet. It took me some time to calm down. I was trembling like a falling leaf. A short time later my heart rate was back to near normal and the Spitfire was safely delivered. When I landed I found Flt Lt Saunders already there waiting to fly me back in a Dominie twin-engined biplane. I had a strange tale to tell him. After this, I never wore goggles again.

During that first week I also piloted Defiants and Hurricanes, but thankfully none of the others lived up to the excitement of my second Spitfire flight. The interesting thing about working on the Delivery Flight was that I got to visit so many other aerodromes and talk to people from different squadrons, which widened my appreciation of the scale of the RAF and its operations. On 12th February I was asked to deliver a Defiant 4III to East Fortune, near Edinburgh, but on the way the weather turned nasty so I took refuge at Derby aerodrome. I was interested to see that they were training glider-pilots here for the Army, using the Magister. I spent a comfortable night at Repton College nearby, and woke in the morning to a white-over from an overnight snowstorm. To my delight the weather improved enough for me to set off again after breakfast. On the way I stopped to refuel at Scampton, the famous bomber station. Here it was a nice day weather-wise, but there was nothing but gloom at this aerodrome. The apron was littered with recently damaged aircraft and I was told the alarming details by one of the officers in the Control Tower as I waited for my own aircraft: a few days previously, several bomber crews had suffered heavy casualties whilst flying Avro Manchesters on a bombing mission over the English Channel when attempting to stop the German battleships

Sharnhorst and *Gneisneau* and their huge convoy returning to the Baltic through the Straits of Dover. Apparently the fire power from these ships had been devastating. 42 British aircraft were lost altogether in a failed attempt to halt the convoy.

From here I travelled by train to Lossiemouth in Scotland and picked up a brand new Hurricane IIc which I duly delivered to Hibaldstow in Lincolnshire. The Dominie picked me up and returned me to High Ercall. On the following day, February 15th, I was told to deliver a new Defiant to my own squadron, which I picked up from Shawbury. My stay with No. 3 Delivery Flight was to end with this delivery and as I set out I was looking forward very much to being back with my pals at 256 again and catching up on what had been happening in my absence.

But on returning to Squires Gate in mid February, I was given a shocking piece of news the moment I entered the Flight hut. Flt Lt Toone was organising the afternoon NFTs and the instant he finished, he came over and took me to one side.

'Sit down, Bryan,' he said. 'I'm afraid I've some very bad news for you. There's no easy way to break it to you. There's been a terrible accident. Ack Greenwood is dead.' I was in such shock that I hardly took in the rest of what he was saying. Apparently Ack had been paired as gunner to Pilot Officer Olney when the Defiant they were flying crashed into the sea along the shoreline off Lytham St Anne's. In conjunction with the army, the Squadron had been carrying out low-flying mock attacks on a coastal defence battery, when Olney turned too steeply and a wing tip touched the water. It appeared also that there was some irregularity in the area he had been flying. Several of the boys saw it happen. The word in the Mess was that Olney was showing off at the time, but of course I wasn't there to have witnessed it first-hand. There was a place called Fairhaven Lake along the shoreline, like a little lagoon. A civvy walking along the front at the time said he thought the plane was acting strangely, 'messing about'. It was not attacking the coastal battery but 'beating up' the house boat at the Lake when the pilot banked too steeply. The wingtip hit the water and the aircraft cartwheeled before crashing nose first into the sand. Olney and Ack were killed outright. Of the two airmen, only Ack's body was able to be recovered from the wreckage. This dreadful incident had happened on February 7th, the same day I had taken up my first Spitfire at High Ercall. On 11th February, while I was still away, Ack's coffin had been sent by train to his family in Hessle, Hull, for burial. Almost inevitably, there was a lurking feeling with me that if I hadn't been away on the Delivery Flight at the time, Ack would have flown with me for the exercise, and he might still be alive. But I knew I couldn't dwell on that. Even so, the whole thing hit me very hard. I was terribly upset and inconsolable. I had fostered a great deal of respect for the Australian, and he had been a bit like a father to me. Nobody could have met a nicer man than Ack Greenwood. It would take a great deal of time before I could come to terms with this tragedy.

More bad news was to follow. During this same month of February 1942, another dreadful and bizarre accident took place on the aerodrome itself. Three aircrew of 256 Squadron, gunner Sgt Carr, Sgt Dove, and Sgt Robinson were walking round the perimeter track from the main gate towards our 'A' Flight dispersal hut, when Sgt Plt Johnny Newall in a small car stopped and offered them a lift. Sgt Robinson decided to walk, but the others accepted. Through a misjudgement by the driver, the car collided head on with a Defiant being piloted by Plt Off. Johnny Tweedale as he was taxying out of the sand-bagged enclosure of a bomb bay. The car was smashed by the propeller and Sgt Carr in the front passenger seat was killed outright. Sgt Dove lost three fingers off his right hand, his face was disfigured by a cut from the propeller and he also suffered a broken thigh. Johnny Newall was at first thought to be suffering from shock, but later was discovered to have broken his neck. Fortunately, these two surviving airmen recovered after several months in hospital. Dove even flew again. Newall spent several weeks in a plaster-cast collar but eventually recovered completely.

As if that wasn't enough, the following day, Peter Harrison-Yates and his gunner, Sgt Woodford had to bale out over Blackpool, but were quite safe.

Naturally enough, we all felt a bit rattled, but the routine carried on. I found it hard to settle. The time seemed disjointed. For the next few weeks Sgt Squires (nicknamed 'Red' because of his ginger hair), who had been the unfortunate Sgt Dove's gunner, teamed up with me, and we got on fine. He came from Leyland near Preston and many a time we used to fly over his place and I would also 'visit' Bolton in the same way. On the 22nd March I was sent down to Watchfield near Swindon on the Blind Approach course, using 'L' for 'Lorenz'. I was there for seven days, and I quite enjoyed myself. On returning back to the old Squadron we got down once more to the old training. I was surprised one day when Flt Lt Toone asked me if I would like to learn to fly the Miles Magister, a small single-engined, two-seater monoplane trainer, which most squadrons had available as a general 'fly-about', invaluable when certain personnel needed to visit other aerodromes for one reason or another. I wasn't even asked to have dual instruction. Toone stood at the side of the cockpit and told me what the various controls and instruments were; then, after Plt Off. Pratt took me up in a short demo flight, we swapped seats and off I went. The thirty-minute solo on 13th April 1942 was completed with ease. I found it very pleasing to fly. I also managed to get a spot of dual instruction in a Botha. My routine was broken again when on 16th April, Red was posted to Bomber command and once again I was without a partner. Any gunner flew with me: Sgt Hollinrake, Sgt Woodford, Sgt Judd, Sgt Clarke, Sgt Robinson, Sgt Green. Sqn Ldr Deanesley left the Squadron in April to be replaced by Wng Cdr J. S. Adams, and during early May, a new Flight Commander arrived ostensibly to organise the coming switch to Beaufighters. He was Sqn Ldr Rabone, DFC, a New Zealander, and quite a well-known ace fighter pilot. For a while he replaced Don Toone as 'A' Flight's boss. Almost at once, the Beaus started to arrive in ones and twos, and several of the resident pilots started their training flights on this aircraft, having already gained training hours on the Oxford and Blenheim.

May 19th 1942 was one of those days I remember as a good day for me. In the morning I went up as passenger in a Beau flown by Wg Cdr Adams. I stood behind him in the well in order to watch and listen to his instructions on how to fly the Beau. I felt excited to be up at last in the latest twin-engined night-fighter. On landing he called me over and told me he was going to recommend me for a commission. I was staggered.

Then in the afternoon I was very pleased to find that because I had already completed a course on Oxfords at South Cerney, I was to by-pass the Oxford and have a dual flight with Rabone in Blenheim No. L6730. A Beaufighter and a Blenheim in one day! This flight lasted for 01.35,

Sgt. 'Red' Squires (gunner) 256 Squadron, flew with Bryan Wild on Defiants for a while after the death of 'Ack' Greenwood and before Wild teamed up with Ralph Gibbons.

and I felt thankful for the thorough training session. Rabone allowed me to handle the aircraft most of the time, including several circuits and landings. He was obviously satisfied with me, and told me I could go solo the next day, which I did with ease. Sgt 'Phil' Austin came with me for the first time. The next few days were spent in becoming experienced on the Blenheim, confirming my good opinion of its qualities: I found it easy to fly and most enjoyable. For the next week I made seven more sorties on the Blenheim, Sgt Austin flying with me all the time. There was no radar on board, so Austin was acting as a navigator. On one of the trips on a lovely, warm Spring day, I and my 'new' Radar Operator flew north to the Lake District, where I put the Blenheim through its paces over the Lakes. It was great fun low-flying over Lake Windermere. During this spell with the Blenheims, I was drafted in as an instructor because I had some experience flying Oxfords. My first 'pupil' was Plt Off. Oxlade, who went solo after two landings. Sgt Jeffs and Plt Off. Yates also received tuition. It felt strange to be on the instructor side of training for a change.

I had been so busy with this routine that I had not had any time to myself to inspect the Beaufighter, apart from that first passenger flight. Wg Cdr Adams now moved things along. After checking on my progress on Blenheims, he suggested it was time I went solo in the Beau, and on May 31st Rabone told me to spend the morning going over the aircraft 'with a

Oxford trainer, Squires Gate, March 1942 Number ?W6557. The Oxford was used to train pilots converting from single-engine fighters to twin-engined flying.

fine toothcomb', as he put it. Then, in the afternoon, I would get airborne, with my Flight Commander standing in the 'well' directly behind me while I was being shown how to fly it.

With a copy of the Beaufighter's notes in my hand, I walked out of the flight hut to Beaufighter No. 7651 not far away on the apron. As usual with a new aircraft, I found the close up view of the plane to be rather awe-inspiring. I had seen these around for some days now but this was the first chance to stand under a wing and touch it. I had digested some of the statistics: 42 feet in length; even longer wingspan 58 feet; weight loaded, about 10 tons. The short snub nose gave it a bulldog look, and the two large radial Bristol Hercules engines, jutting forward from the leading edge of the wings to a point beyond the nose, gave the impression that it couldn't wait to get 'off the lead'. A sturdy undercarriage lifted the main fuselage. At a middle point was the radio operator's cupola, a blister of clear Perspex which enabled the second member of the crew to obtain an all-round view. On take-off, the observer sat with his back to the pilot, and as the Beau's terrific acceleration built up, the view towards the tail and beyond was an exciting experience. This I discovered later when I had occasion to be a passenger in that central seat.

I couldn't wait to climb into the cockpit. I found the entrance was somewhat unique. A hatch-door with a short ladder extension slotted snugly to the underside of the fuselage when closed. This was situated behind the undercart bays. The door was hinged at a halfway point and when it was off the catch it swung upward into a space behind the cockpit called the 'well', leaving it locked a vertical position with the ladder below the fuselage. I climbed into the well, closing the door as I did so and this sealed the entrance. I turned to look back all the way to the tail end of the aircraft. The RO's swivel seat was facing the tail at the moment. In front of that seat and facing me I could see the small radar screen. Taking up a large area of this middle floor space where I stood were the ammunition feed cases and breech blocks of the four Hispano Suiza 20 mm cannons whose very long barrels ran the length of the fuselage from midway to the nose. Outside, the four gun ports could be seen with protective gauze. To get into the cockpit I had to reach up to grasp two horizontal bars fixed to the roof and lying lengthwise. The seat was already 'collapsed' with my parachute in the bucket part of the unit. Like a gymnast, I had to haul myself up and then forward, feet first, sliding into the waiting seat, which was hinged and in two parts. At the touch of a lever, I made the seat 'sit up'. The exit procedure, of course, would be exactly the opposite. Everything about this aircraft, I thought, was 'solid', which seems an odd word to use in reference to a fighter aircraft. The wings were long, and had a cross section at the fuselage joint which was amazingly thick. The petrol tanks were embedded in these spacious wings, along with six .303 Browning machine guns.

The cockpit was roomy and the large side windows, free from bars on either side, gave me a wonderful outlook above and along the wings. Most pilots who sat in the front for the first time were astounded at this new freedom of vision, after the confined cockpits and restricted view of most fighter planes. From a night-fighter pilot's point of view, this improvement in forward vision, from Defiant to Beau, was remarkable. Flying almost blind in the dark, you wanted the best view you could possibly have of what might be coming at you. The windscreen was of bullet-proof glass, 2″ thick, and the gun sight was housed here. Reassuringly, I noted that the curved roof window was hinged to enable me to climb out that way in case of emergency. Facing me was the extensive instrument panel and control units, plus the usual gauges all in duplicate. The control column was a 'butterfly' wheel, with a gun button, camera button and the brake lever. At my feet was the foot control for the rudder. I tested it: it seemed heavy. I reminded myself that rudder control would be a vital factor on take-off, remembering something an experienced Beaufighter pilot had once said with reference to this aircraft having a habit of swinging on take-off.

At 2 o'clock that same day, I was standing in the well of Beau No. 7651 behind my tutor, Sqn Ldr Rabone, just off the end of the runway all set

Beaufighter cockpit: "Facing me was the extensive instrument panel and control units, plus the usual gauges all in duplicate, of course. The control column was a 'butterfly' wheel, with a gun button, camera button and the brake lever. At my feet was the foot control for the rudder."

for take-off. Rabone spoke aloud on the intercom as he went through the cockpit drill, then turned the aircraft slowly to edge onto the runway itself. With brakes on, the engines were revved up for a few seconds, then, with the brakes off, the two throttles were moved forward through the slots and the plane surged ahead at speed. I was astonished at the force of the acceleration. I listened to the pilot: 'Get the tail up as soon as you can—you'll soon get the hang of it. There! She's up. Speed around sixty. There's a slight swing to starboard, d'ye see? Correct it with rudder and edge forward slightly the starboard throttle ... all done gently, mark you. Here she comes off the deck. Speed nearing a hundred ... ease stick back, increase throttle ...' I listened intently as the Beau climbed rapidly to around 1,000 feet or more. For the next twenty minutes, Rabone cruised around doing turns, diving and climbing and generally putting the plane through its paces. Then he landed, repeated the take-off, and then landed once more, before stepping out of the aircraft to hand it over to me for my first solo. I had no difficulty with this flight. I found the plane very similar to its sister aircraft, the Blenheim. There was actually very little swing on take-off. Rabone had told me that it varied with each plane. The landing wasn't perfect: I realised that I had been too high just before touch-down.

That evening I filled in the monthly summary in my log book ready for the CO and Flight Commander to sign the next day. My last entry for May was: Beaufighter 7651. First solo. Time airborne 1.05.

The Beaufighter was a marvellous aircraft. Powered by the two Bristol radial engines, it proved to be tremendously fast compared to the old Defiant. And the firing power was tremendous. I kept marvelling at it: four cannons in the fuselage and six machine guns in the wing! Unlike the Defiant, it was actually equipped with radar. No distant 'Control' on the ground to relay fixings but my own radio operator in the cupola who could also see in real time what was happening. The Beaufighter would prove to be one of the most versatile twin-engined fighters in the RAF, used as a bomber or fighter, and to drop torpedoes in Coastal Command. Its duration was over five hours and extremely reliable. It weighed ten tons. It made me feel both safer and better-equipped for fighting than any previous plane I had flown. My last trip in the good old Defiant was with Sgt Green on May 15th, and I was rather sorry that I made an awful landing.

With the coming of the Beaufighters, my life felt much more settled. Life in the RAF was never static, however. There was a certain amount of sadness in the Sergeants' Mess that very evening as most of the gunners were being posted to Bomber Command. One or two had opted to take a radar operators' course to enable them to switch to Beaus, and my friend Deryk Hollinrake was one of these.

My time at Squires Gate was coming to an end. On the 5th June 1942, the Squadron transferred to Woodvale on the coast near Southport. I flew there that day in 'G', my fifth trip on Beaus. The squadron's duties were the same: to protect Liverpool, Manchester and Belfast from night attacks. The Polish 315 Squadron, equipped with the Spitfire VB and VC, had been based at the aerodrome from April 1942 to defend the skies in daylight.

Blackpool had been very good to us and the night before we had made a point of saying goodbye to it in style. But this move to Southport pleased me. It was even nearer to home for me than Squires Gate and this mattered particularly at the moment because my motorbike had just conked out. I liked our new station right from the start. The food was good, and it was easy to travel the seven miles to Southport on an electric tram that took about eight minutes. It didn't take us long to explore the town, and 'Matti and Tissots' was quickly established as the best café. The most popular pubs were the Queens, Royal, Prince of Wales. Other little dives included Dorothy's Club, and a night club just off the main road on Ford Street. A Sergeants' Mess dance was held every Sunday in the Mess, and on one Saturday in the month the Mess threw a big dance. We were allowed to invite people from outside, so as can well be imagined, the Sergeants' Mess was very popular with most of the boys. It was at one of these dances I met Mr and Mrs Edwards and their twin daughters, Jessamine and Pauline. These people invited one or two of us to their house in return, and we became very firm friends. I was going to miss my cricket, however. While at Squires Gate I had been a guest player occasionally for Fleetwood Cricket Club and also St Anne's C.C.

I was still Flight Sergeant, so my membership of the Sergeants Mess continued for some time until my commission should become valid in September. The observers were a great crowd of chaps: Sgt Mattingly (Mate) flew with Flt Lt Alan Strachan. 'Dowei' flew with Sgt Dave Cotterill, and Patterson (Pat) flew with Plt Off. Peter Harrison-Yates. I managed to get home to Bolton every odd day or so. I always went by train, a journey of around 45 minutes, as the bike was still being repaired. While home on one of these days, I met a girl called Joan Berry down at the Club and saw her most times when I was home. My brothers Alan and Frank sometimes managed to get home when I was there so we had quite a good time. On June 14th my young cousin Roy came to the camp and asked for a trip. With a bit of wangling I managed to get him up in the Magister. He enjoyed himself, but was beginning to feel a little queer. He finished up his day by having a grand tea as a guest to the Mess. All this contact with home meant a lot to me and I made the most of it, as I knew it couldn't last for ever.

By this time I had made several trips in the Beau, training on beacon homings and cross-country runs with Sgt Phil Austin as my RO. As June passed, Austin and I started to pile the hours up on the Beau, each trip averaging out around two hours. A great deal of these day flights were concentrated on AI practice (Aircraft Interception with Radar), but it wasn't until June 25th that we actually made our first night flight lasting 1.40 minutes, under the heading of 'Dusk Landings and Local Flying'. By this time I loved the Beau. I found it very easy to fly and amazingly manoeuvrable for its size.

Austin and I were also becoming au fait with Beaufighter radar interceptions. It was clear to me that their success depended to some measure on the skill of the RO. There was a sequence of stages in the whole process. In a sector operations room the course of enemy bombers would be plotted. The controller would allocate certain of these raids to other controllers at the new radar stations, known as ground controlled interception. This radar controller, after picking up an intruder on the screen (a blip), would summon a night fighter to engage the enemy. In most cases this fighter would be in the air already, on patrol. The fighter would be vectored to the area of the 'bandit', but it was imperative to get the Beau there in the right position to carry out an attack, which was to be astern of the enemy. The idea was to turn the Beau onto the same vector as the bandit and close on him from about two or three miles away. At this point, the RO would spot the blip on his small radar screen. Then, by direct and immediate intercommunication with the pilot, the RO would issue directions and orders to his colleague to close in on the bandit, the ideal position being just below, out of range of the enemy's guns; and behind in order to catch up with him. The snag was that the forward range of the radar corresponded to the height of the aircraft above ground. So, if the Beau was only 3,000 feet up, the radar only picked up the blip if it was within 3,000-foot range. If the Beau was at 10,000 feet, its range was better. Later, the Germans found out about this and started their bombing runs low down to escape detection from Beaufighters. Later still, we brought out the 'long-nosed' Beau whose radar overcame this discrepancy. After all this, only when the pilot could actually see the enemy with his own eyes could he manoeuvre the Beau into a firing position. On moonlit nights this would not be too difficult, but on pitch black nights the Beau could be almost on top of the bandit but perhaps would still not spot it. The enemy would have a gunner on the watch, but he too would have some difficulty picking out a stalking aircraft. However, we knew that once the Beau was in the correct firing position, the fire power of the four cannons and six machine guns was usually fatal for the intruder.

Towards the end of June I was interviewed by Grp Cpt MacDonald for my commission. Everything appeared OK.

I was still not settled with a radio operator. I'm afraid that by this time my relations with Sgt Austin weren't very good, and on July 11th he had his last 'flip' with me. His posting was generally expected. Sgt Ralph Gibbons' pilot, McGarry, was posted onto Defiants again, so Ralph volunteered to fly with me. Once again I was pleasantly teamed up with someone a lot older than myself. Ralph Gibbons was aged 33 and married, with two children. He was a teacher in 'civvy' street, and a B.Sc. to boot.

I was now operational on Beaufighters, but training still went on with Ground Interception (GI) or Air Interception (AI) practice during the day and GCI practice at night. During these months, there were many 'Bullseye' exercises, day and night. In these, Bomber Command sent their Lancasters, Wellingtons and Halifaxes to various parts of the region so that the night-fighters could gain practice in interception by radar. It was also good practice for the bombers, offering the chance for their gunners to 'return fire' and their pilots to take evasive action.

For me there were the usual succession of small incidents. On July 18th, Ralph and I took the Oxford down to Middle Wallop to collect spares, but met terrible weather on the return journey. We had to lob down at Stratford after flying in pouring rain for thirty minutes, only just being able to see the deck. We got back to base in one piece, eventually.

On the night of July 27th 1942, after Phil Austin had been posted to another squadron, Ralph and I were called to our first operational interception. We were scrambled to look for an intruder edging towards the Liverpool area. At a height of around 5,000 feet, on a bad night of rain and cloud, we actually saw a Junkers 88, well below us. Unfortunately, it was travelling in the opposite direction and at some speed, and by the time I had dived and turned to pursue it, the enemy was far ahead. Radar Control gave me a revised compass heading, but although all the stops were pulled, the Ju 88 fled from the scene. It must have been aware that it had been picked up on radar and decided to call it a night.

On August 10th, I experienced a very unpleasant and alarming event. On a day when I was due home on leave, I was involved in an air-to-ground firing exercise. The official target was an old wreck way out on the vast sandbanks off Southport Pier. I started the run in from the land to fire at the wreck: for safety reasons the line of approach was heading out to sea. Just as I started firing with my four cannons and six machine guns, I saw three children running out from the opposite side of the wreck; they must have been sheltering under the hull. I was completely horrified. Were there any more down there? Had I hit anyone? I was thoroughly shaken, but fortunately I learnt later that no one was hurt because my firing was slightly off target. Phew!

Over the summer there were several comings and goings. Sqn Ldr Rabone was posted to another squadron in June, and his place was taken by a Sqn

Ldr Roger de W. K. Winlaw and his Radio Operator (RO), Plt Off. Claude 'Cyril' Ashton. Both were famous. Roger Winlaw was a double Cambridge blue, and played cricket for Sussex. Ashton was a triple Cambridge blue. He was an English Amateur International at football, and he played for Corinthians. He also played cricket for Sussex. They were both extremely popular and very well liked. As can be imagined, our cricket eleven was pretty good. I used to play wicket-keeper and got quite a lot of useful tips off both of them. Cyril Ashton and I were close friends and as well as playing with him in the Squadron cricket and football teams, we used to play chess together. In August, Wg Cdr Adams was posted, and the new Commanding Officer was Wg Cdr Hayes, DFC. Another newcomer to the Squadron was Flg Off. Allan, the former Sgt Allan who was my instructor on Tiger Moths.

Later that month, on a day flight, I had to carry out my first ever forced landing on a Beaufighter when the reduction gear packed up and one engine went into full revs before cutting out. We were above cloud at about 8,000 feet, but we got down in one piece. On another occasion on October 24th, while doing an NFT on Johnny Tweedale's old 'C', the starboard engine cut, and I forced landed OK at Calverley, not far from Crewe. Johnny had to come later in the day and pick me and Ralph up in his brand new Beau VI. I had several operational scrambles but nothing came of them. In terms of operational flights, the last few months of 1942 petered out with uneventful patrols, with no sight of the enemy.

But there was plenty happening every day and I never felt bored. On Sept 1st, I went on leave, and while I was there a telegram arrived saying that my commission was through and that clothing coupons would be sent on the next day. My brother Alan was also on leave, and he and my cousin Roy travelled with me to get my Pilot Officer's uniform from Moss Bros. in Manchester. Immediately on return I took my friend Aircraftwoman (ACW) Jean Alexander up for a trip in a Magister. I circled over the Club at Bolton, and could see a lot of folks on the bowling green. On another occasion I flew as passenger with Plt Off. Robinson, who dropped in at Shawbury for me to see my brother, Frank, who was RAF ground crew. On my return to Southport I now moved into officers' quarters in a large house at Ainsdale about two miles from the aerodrome. One evening in October, after several of us had been into Southport, we returned late to the house, to find when we opened the front door that the hall was full of sand. Then we suddenly realised why. Flt Lt Alan Strachan was standing at the top of the stairs, obviously in one of his drunken moods, and was hurling sandbags down the stairs. The amazing thing was that this officer, an experienced and very likeable pilot, was the mildest of men when sober. Later on in the war I learnt that he had been court-martialled for hurling furniture out of a bedroom in a famous hotel in Valetta, Malta.

At the very end of October the Squadron received another terrible blow. It happened on a night 'bullseye' exercise over Bangor in which Lancasters and Wellingtons were being 'intercepted'. Sqn Ldr Roger Winlaw with Plt Off. Cyril Ashton in their Beaufighter collided with a Wellington bomber in mid-air. The two 256 Squadron aircrew were killed as well as the entire crew of the bomber. It hit us all very hard and once again I had lost a very close friend, not to the enemy but an accident on training exercise. One night in December brought this incident poignantly to my mind when on a moonlight training exercise we successfully intercepted a Lancaster. Believe me, a Lancaster, close up, is an astounding sight in the moonlight. Given the difficulties of interception in the dark, these exercises were dangerous indeed.

In November I had been given a new Beau Mk VI to look after, 'L' for 'London'. She was a straight-tailed job, while all the others had dihedral tails. She was a beauty, and flew like a rocket. I really looked after that machine and thought of her as 'mine'. On December 7th, Ralph Gibbons and I flew 'L' on detachment to Ballyhalbert, near Bangor in Northern Ireland. We were there for a week only, as a 'stand-in' for 153 Squadron who were being posted overseas. (Later, I and Joe Berry would be posted overseas to join this Squadron).

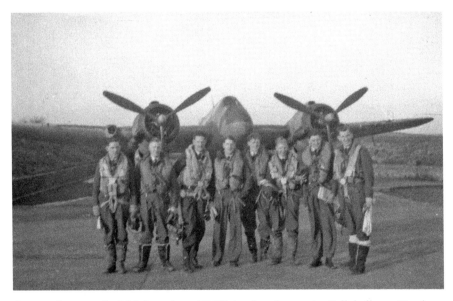

Group photograph, 256 Squadron 'A' Flight detachment in Ballyhalbert, Northern Ireland, standing in for 153 Squadron. Bryan Wild 5th from left; Ralph Gibbons on left of group. Joe Berry and Ian Watson stayed in Woodvale, carrying out NFT testing, and had some days' leave.

Beaufighter JT-L, EL158, 256 Squadron, Woodvale 1942. Bryan Wild: 'She was a beauty, and flew like a rocket. I really looked after that machine and thought of her as "mine"'. Wild and Gibbons flew her on detachment to Northern Ireland in December 1942.

256 Squadron Beaufighter, JT-G X8016 (photographed from Beau JT-L EL158 flown by Bryan Wild and Ralph Gibbons on detachment Northern Ireland, December 1942). Built by Bristols at Weston-super-Mare. Joined 307 Polish Squadron, then 256, after which she went to Middle East 89 Squadron. She was scrapped in June 1945. *Aircraft history detail supplied by Russell Brown*

I returned to Squires Gate on Dec 19th 1942 to find the station preparing for a bumper Christmas. In the mess we heard the sobering parcel of news that all our gunners of Defiants who transferred out of the Squadron were now missing on Bomber Command, except Sgt Harris, who was reported to be a prisoner of war. Fred House had died in June, shot down in a Whitney V bomber over Hamburg. I was also extremely sad to learn that my close friend in Canada, Tommy Hunter, was killed early on in his flying career, not that long after he left us, on a 'Whirlwind' fighter. I didn't know the details.

Meanwhile, the life of the Squadron went on and we had Christmas to enjoy. On Christmas morning the Officers went over to the Sergeants Mess at 10.30 a.m. for a few drinks; then the Sergeants came over to our Mess at 11.00. Noon arrived, and we all went over to the Airmen's Mess and served the airmen with the best Christmas dinner I had seen in the Forces to that date. We returned at 2.30 and had ours, all feeling a little merry. In the evening, Sqn Ldr Mackie, Don Toone, Plt Off. Robinson, Johnny Tweedale and myself were guests of Mr and Mrs Forster, a director of the De Havilland firm at Lostock, near Bolton, who had invited us to spend Christmas night with them. We had quite a nice time, but not enough excitement, we thought. On Boxing Day, the CO asked me if I would like to go abroad with Ralph Gibbons. Joe Berry and his RO Ian Watson would also be going. That was excitement! After thinking it over, I consented and Ralph and I were medically examined that afternoon and inoculated. It all happened very quickly. The next day I was inoculated again at West Kirby, this time for yellow fever, and said my goodbyes to 256. I was sent home on leave over New Year. Friday 1st January 1943 was my last day at home before going abroad and there were more goodbyes to be said. I went for a walk with my friend Joan in the afternoon and at night went to the Club for a farewell dance, leaving at 1230. I wondered when—and, in a smaller inner voice, if—I would be back.

6

Sweeping up
the Mediterranean

From 1940 there had been fighting in North and East Africa, as Italy tried to realise its ambitions to establish a new empire among the old European colonies. Germany moved its Afrika Korps troops and tanks into the region in early 1941 and the fighting ranged back and forth throughout the territory. Hitler also attacked Russia in June 1941 and the Balkan states were in turmoil, with internal uprisings of their own adding to the destabilisation there. However, on 7 December 1941, the Japanese attacked the US fleet at Pearl Harbor, and America entered the war. By the end of the following summer, Rommel's forces, hampered generally by lack of supplies and equipment and with insufficient air support, had retreated to high ground near Alamein in Egypt, West of Alexandria. With new Sherman tanks and tactical air cover in support, General Montgomery's British forces won the ensuing battle and in the months that followed, Rommel retreated west, only to be trapped between the advance of the 8th Army and the Anglo-American troops which had landed in Algeria and Morocco in Operation Torch in November 1942. El Alamein was a turning point of which Churchill famously said, 'This is not the end. It is not even the beginning of the end. But it is, perhaps, the end of the beginning.'

Three days before Wild and Gibbons arrived in North Africa on 26 January 1943, the 8th Army captured Tripoli, but the campaign for Tunisia continued into May. All this while, control of the Mediterranean was vital in ensuring Allied supplies reached their armies and the movement of Axis troops and equipment was prevented.

Around six o'clock the next evening, 2nd January 1943, Ralph and I arrived at Lyneham near Swindon to find Joe Berry and Ian Watson were there already. Ralph was a Non-Commissioned Officer (NCO), so he was in the Sergeants' Quarters. After Ralph had gone to find his billet, I joined Joe at the bar. 'What's it like here, then?' I asked him, hopefully. He shook his head and smiled ruefully, 'It's pretty bad, Bryan; brace yourself. The food's awful and the quarters are damned cold. But hopefully they'll get the postings sorted out quickly.' We had not yet been assigned to any Squadron and we hoped to find out more about our destination the next day.

Sure enough, we were soon being briefed for our trip to North Africa, where we learned we would be sent initially to a 'pilots' pool' to await posting to one of three squadrons. We were issued with tropical gear and miscellaneous items such as flasks, escape aids, desert survival pack, leaflets in Arabic and money.

On 7th January, along with ten other crews including Joe Berry and Ian Watson, Ralph and I went by coach to Filton near Bristol to collect a brand new Beaufighter from the factory: no. V8633. It was like taking my old car to a car dealer and then part-exchanging it for a brand new one. I felt sheer delight in flying the plane back to Lyneham. However, the bad weather didn't allow us to carry out the consumption test on it until January 13th: an all-round trip around the coast from Cornwall to Blackpool and beyond that took 5.05 hours. The results were good: petrol consumption 80 gallons per hour; air miles 2.44 per gallon; range 1,448 miles; and the full endurance of the aircraft could be 7 hours 36 minutes. All very pleasing. The kite then went in for inspection, while we waited ... and waited.

Joe had been right about the facilities at Lyneham. It was a depressing place, dingy and cold, but we were forced to spend a lot of time here as the worst weather for years clamped down on us for days on end, with rain, sleet, snow and, gales. On one attempt to reach Portreath, our starting point for Gibraltar, we had to return, but couldn't face that Mess again, so diverted to Hullavington, the Central Flying School for instructors: an inspired move. The Mess was full of rings and DFCs and we were given a wonderful meal and a cosy room. Breakfast was a grand affair, in a classy Mess where everything was spick and span. 'It has to be,' said Ralph, 'With all these wing commanders knocking around.' We finally joined the rest of the boys at Portreath on 21st January.

We put navigation equipment in stores, signed the usual 'bumph papers', collected all the gen on RT procedure, studied photos of Portuguese ports and Gibraltar approaches and felt fired up and ready to go. Ralph spent ages messing around with his navigation stuff and plotting courses for the trip. But the weather kept us grounded.

I was shaken awake at 4.30 in the morning of 24th January. It was dark and cold. 'Weather's OK,' said a voice, as I sat up in bed. 'You're all off!' We were told to go across Portugal, down the border of Portugal and Spain. '5/10 cloud till halfway and then clear', the Met. said.

We were all airborne about 6.00 a.m., but shortly after leaving Lands End, our RT packed up. The IFF (Identification Friend or Foe radar signalling) blew up, and the petrol cover flew open, so we returned. The message came through later that all the rest had reached 'Gib' safely.

The next day we were feeling rather down. Our kite was ready to go but the Met. said a front was expected the next day so we wouldn't be going then either. We wandered into the village. Nearly all the locals were closed, it being a Monday, and we had to be satisfied with the remaining two dives. We came back on the liberty. I was not feeling too good, and looked forward to having a hangover in the morning.

4.30 in the morning, dark and cold, and once again I was shaken awake. 'Weather's OK,' said a voice, as I sat up in bed. 'You're off!' I groaned and turned over. 'Go away! Leave me alone!' I was shaken again, more roughly this time. 'Get up, you idiot, you're off, I tell you! The Met. was wrong: the weather's going to be OK today.'

Ralph shook his head when we saw me. 'You look rough!'

'I'll be OK,' I said. I looked gloomily up at the sky. 'Which is more than I'd like to say for the weather.'

'It doesn't look too good, does it?' said Ralph. 'Low cloud and continuous rain. Not what I'd call wonderful for flying, but apparently it should get better as we go.'

Ralph and I set off into very grey skies, heading for warmer climes. We were told to climb to 20,000 feet, above the front. At 1,000 feet we were in cloud, but once we had climbed through it to about 10,000 feet, a flood of relief came over us to see the sun rise to our port side. Though I was so pleased to see it, I averted my gaze from its bright rays. I didn't feel too good. I had a stabbing headache and my mouth felt dry as dust. Even so it was a sweet flight. We cruised at about 12,000 feet above cloud all the way to the middle of Portugal. Ralph Gibbons' navigation was almost spot-on here, only five miles adrift off the track on the first pin point. Ralph brought me a flask of tea to celebrate. Boy, it tasted good! By the time I'd finished sipping my tea, we were nearing the Coast of Spain, where we changed course for Gibraltar and I changed tanks. My hangover had receded and my spirits rose with the rapid rise in temperature. I managed to wriggle out of some of my thick flying clothes. We landed safely at Gibraltar on a fine, warm morning, the whole trip taking 5.15 hours.

This day, 26 January 1943, felt quite a historic day for me and I was brimming with excitement. That night Ralph and I went sightseeing. We were amazed to find searchlights all over the place and the whole town lit up. After the freezing cold of a British winter, the evening felt luxuriously warm, and we sauntered around feeling very relaxed with our hands in our pockets.

Back at base the next day we looked again at the scores of different aircraft packed onto the aerodrome, some of them American. Liberators,

Hudsons, Wellingtons and Spitfires littered the place along with the Beaufighters. The heat coming up from the ground and beating down from above was terrific. In midmorning we were briefed for the next leg of the journey to Maison Blanche Aerodrome, Algiers, North Africa. This French Colony and the surrounding coastal area from Tunis to Tangier had been captured by the Americans the previous summer with Operation Torch.

We were airborne before lunch for the long trip across the Mediterranean and Ralph took a farewell camera shot of the Rock of Gibraltar from the astro-hatch as we set out over the blue sea. We landed safely dead on course at Maison Blanche 2.30 hours later. We learned that the rest of the boys were at Setif, 200 miles further east, and after a short refuelling break, we set off to follow them. We passed ranges of mountains 7,000 feet above sea level, an awesome sight stretching out below us, sharp-edged with shadows and vivid sunlight. Finally we came in towards Setif, a small town set in the heart of the Atlas Mountains at 3,000 feet above sea level. A grass 'drome, no runways. My landing was OK but it was very bumpy across the grass before we jolted to a halt and parked the Beau. We lost no time in heading into town about seven miles away to meet up with the other boys and report to the transit house, a large, comfortable building which was once a senior girls school. Within days all the crews from Portreath were billeted here awaiting posting to one of the three squadrons: 153 Squadron based at Maison Blanche; 600 Squadron at Bone, further east near the Tunisian border; and 255 Squadron here at Setif. Setif was much cooler than Maison Blanche on the plains of Algiers. We put loads of extra blankets on our beds the first night. The Mess was in one of the old classrooms and the food seemed to match the surroundings. Most of the officers including the CO here belonged to the Aircraft Storage Unit (ASU), a very nice bunch of chaps. It was a strange atmosphere, with so many people in this transit pool not knowing where or when they would be posted.

Setif was very much a French-speaking town. I only knew a very little French. I didn't mind that inconvenience at first, as I expected to be moved out the next day or so, but in the event we had to hang around here for nearly three weeks before Ralph and I were back to flying duties. All the aircrew fumed at being locked here in inaction once again and we vented our immense frustration by hitting the town. Ralph, Joe, Ian and I wandered around the bars in the early evenings. There were plenty of cheap wines and other drinks to be had, and I think I tried them all: muscatel, Alicante, cheap vin de table, vermouth and the like. Very nice they were, too, but I was told to be careful. 'Go easy, old chap,' someone said to me, 'Terrific hangover results, if you're not careful.' We were also officially warned to steer clear of the town's brothel.

Four days into my time at Setif I went down with a bad cold and a touch of tonsillitis, probably due to the change in climate and the poor heating at the School. My North African campaign was not getting off to the best of starts. There were some high spots, however. The first came in the second week. I visited the 'drome one afternoon and saw a familiar figure standing in the entrance: my old friend Jimmy Ward. I had been to his wedding in November but we hadn't met since, and I was amazed and overjoyed to see him there. Over a drink in the Mess, he told me he had been with 255 Squadron here since they invaded North Africa. 'We've had bags of excitement,' he said, 'But no Huns.' The second compensation was that there were some nice girls around the place. One particularly lovely girl presided over the drinks at the Bar de la Paix, and all the boys were after her. The Paix opened between 5.30 and 7 p.m., a useful bit of the day to be able to fill when you were kicking your heels and staving off boredom.

To save ourselves from becoming too brassed off we put on a concert on 6th February. The entertainment was home-made and a bit cranky, but the bar had been open a while and by the time the show got going we were ready to laugh at anything. I told three Stanley Holloway monologues in my best Bolton accent which the boys seemed to enjoy immensely. Sqn Ldr Greenhough, a Yorkshireman, was tickled to death, it seemed. I came off quite pleased with myself and slept like a top afterwards, but woke up freezing cold in the small hours. Time hung heavy on my hands. On 8th February, some people's postings came through, but I was not one of them. Joe and Ian left for 153 Squadron and Dave Cotterill was posted to 255 Squadron here at Setif, where he paired up with Gordon Sproule, from my old 256 Squadron. Ralph and I were getting even more cheesed off at being left behind, and hearing from Dave Cotterill that he was doing duty pilot in his new Squadron merely rubbed salt into the wound. My cold came back, and so did the snow.

Finally both the weather and our prospects brightened up on 14th February. We were posted to 153 Squadron, Maison Blanche, leaving the next day. This meant we would be reunited with Joe and Ian. To celebrate, we headed out to town to say farewell to the Bar de la Paix. We had a cheerful session there, and at ten minutes after seven we were savouring our last glass when a military policeman walked up to us and took our names for being caught drinking in the Bar minutes after closing time. He lost no time in reporting us, because the next morning I had to report to Wing Commander Kelly, where I can only say I was ticked off in a nice way, as was Ralph. All was well that ended well.

The next day, Ralph and I set off by three-ton truck for Maison Blanche aerodrome, driving through the main east-west spine of the spectacular Atlas Mountains, which we had flown over when we first came to North

Africa. Snow on the tops shone brilliantly in the sunlight. En route, we passed scores of vehicles going east, American and British, on their way to the front in Tunisia where the Germans were preparing to evacuate to Italy. About fifty miles from Algiers, the winding road started to descend to the large plain below. It was now becoming hot in sharp contrast to the coolness of the mountain region, and we passed vineyards and orange groves on either side. We arrived at Maison Blanche at 6.00 p.m. and were driven direct to the Officers Mess just outside the 'drome, a small French colonial-style hotel—called St George, which pleased us greatly. Flt Sgt Ralph Gibbons, of course, joined the other NCO's in the Sergeants' Mess not far away.

I was very pleased to see Joe Berry and Ian Watson there. I caught up with them in the bar. 'What's the gen, Joe?' I asked as he handed me a drink. 'Well, you'll see the CO in the morning,' he answered, 'Wg Cdr Mosely. He can be a bit of a terror at times. There's plenty of action here. Most of the pilots already have 'kills' to their credit because there have been months of raids and attacks on ports and convoys. There are scrambles all the time.' The bar filled up and Joe paused as a group of airmen pushed past us. 'And it's jolly overcrowded,' he continued. 'There are twenty-nine crews here all together. There are so many flights all the time that we have to preserve petrol, so all NFTs are limited to thirty minutes. Ian and I have done three operational hours already, but no fun as yet. The hangars are all in shreds: they were dive-bombed in January, apparently; and there are mine fields all around the place, so watch where you go. I'm afraid you won't get much sleep.'

I soon found he was right about that. No time was wasted in getting the new arrivals on the State of Readiness roster. The following morning, after meeting Wg Cdr. Mosely (without any indications of him being 'a terror' at that moment in time), we were told that we would be on duty immediately for a NFT that afternoon. Just before midday we walked round the aerodrome to get the feel of the place. 153 Squadron's Flight hut was on the opposite side of the 'drome in relation to the main hangars and other buildings. We could see, as Joe had said, that the hangars were now mere shells after the bombing. Nearby was the operational complex of the American Air Force day fighters, equipped with Bell P-39 Airacobras and Lockheed Lightnings, with their unique twin tail booms.

I was put on the programme immediately from that day onwards but the first couple of nights I was way down on the list, so didn't scramble. Dispersal was a hut near the watch tower where ground crew and air crew all slept—or tried to sleep—in the same room. The heat was terrific, and if that wasn't enough to keep me awake, there seemed to be scrambles all the time, which meant that people were coming and going all night long.

Maison Blanche aerodrome, Algiers, February 1943, showing extensive bomb damage to the hangars after raids suffered in January.

1942: American Airacobras on day duty on the Taher airstrip along the North African coast, one of several between Algiers to Tunisia, built by the Americans to protect shipping in the Mediterranean from the Luftwaffe. 153 Squadron night-fighters shared the strips. Taher and Bone in particular were used extensively, allowing the Beaus to spread out along the Mediterranean to be on immediate night call.

No Huns were shot down. I was very grateful to get back to the hotel the following night and I set about making my billet as comfortable as I could. I was sharing with Ian Watson and a Canadian, Nick Carter. The food was good, as it was still prepared and served by the French owners of the hotel.

The next day I felt like exploring and asked Ian for some suggestions. 'Why don't you have a look round Algiers?' he said. 'Hitch-hiking is easy with all the Americans stationed there. They have more cars than they need, especially these 'Jeeps', which are great fun. Algiers is not too bad, but there are only two English-speaking picture houses and they're usually packed to the gunnels. The films are pretty ancient.' He grinned at my expression. Nevertheless I enjoyed my day. There were many friendly Americans around and I soon got a lift in a jeep. As we headed into Algiers we stopped along the way to buy oranges and tangerines, ten for a penny and absolutely delicious. I managed to hitch back easily before dark. I soon discovered one good thing about being posted here: if you were off, you were off. There was no reporting down to the flights. It made the days off more relaxed. They needed to be.

If I had been grumbling in recent months about inactivity, I soon found myself on the opposite track, because in the next few months, there were

153 Squadron aircrew on a wall in Maison Blanche. Joe Berry third from right. Far right, Ken Rayment, who as co-pilot was killed in the Munich air crash of 1958 when many of the Manchester United football team were killed. He was flying the aircraft at the time of the crash and died afterwards of his injuries.

night scrambles and patrols a-plenty. A large number of Allied convoys were passing eastwards through the Mediterranean Sea as the war reached a critical stage in this region. The Luftwaffe, with bases in France and southern Europe generally, were continually attacking this shipping and particularly at night. To cover this large stretch of coast from Algiers to Tunisia, 153 Squadron had the use of airstrips at various inlets along the shore line. Taher and Ddjelli were two examples. These had been erected by the Americans whose Airocobras were on day duty, the night-fighters taking over from dusk till dawn. The landing strips were simply linked flat metal sleepers about twelve feet wide, laid by unrolling them like a huge and lengthy carpet. Because the Atlas Mountains edged right up to the shore on this coast, these strips could only be put down where a river plunged down to the sea, and there were only a few of these. Even these streams had very little flat land either side, so the path of the landing strip was always along the direction of the estuary; in these cases South to North.

To use these safely, pilots could only land or take-off from the land towards the sea, the mountains acting like a brick wall. There was no way a Beaufighter could risk landing there at night, so the plane would be flown there in the afternoon, and, if the fighter was scrambled during the night, the pilot would have to return to Algiers to land. Apart from 153, the two other Squadrons, 600 and 255, were also providing convoy cover, as well as dealing with German intruder aircraft attacking important targets on this coast line.

The routine of the night duty was the same as ever: six aircraft on each of two Flights, 'A' and 'B', each taking two nights on duty, two nights off. It was quite common here to be scrambled again for a second patrol before dawn. I had plenty of operational scrambles in the next few months but I personally had no success. It was not through lack of trying; I just seemed not to be in the right place at the right time. Bad weather conditions often played a big part in deciding whether or not you had a chance of getting a 'visual' on a 'Hun'. It never seemed to fall for me. However, some of the crews, in the right place and at the right time, did manage to engage and destroy the enemy, usually Junkers 88s (Ju 88s) or Heinkels, which were both versatile, medium-sized bombers. Indeed, this squadron had a fine record of victories against intruder aircraft, most of them being shot down before I arrived at the base. On busy spells we all found the pace gruelling; not because of enemy activity, but because of the compounded flying hours of more than one scramble or patrol a night. When this happened on the following night as well, I found myself staggering off to bed the next morning and sleeping in until late in the afternoon, sometimes without having eaten.

Bryan Wild looks out of a Beaufighter cockpit, North Africa 1942.

For example, on Sunday 21st February I was scrambled in the morning at 1000 hours, but had to return because the RT was unserviceable. I then scrambled again in Beau 'O' but the Hun had turned back by the time we arrived on the scene and we pancaked an hour later. I did a half-hour Night Flying Test (NFT) in the afternoon on Beau 'J'. At night I was second on and was scrambled again after a Hun. The night was cloudy: 8/10 cumulus, base 1,000 to 7,000 feet. Ralph and I chased the Hun all over the sea at 800 feet and obtained close pursuit through good ACI but we soon lost him as he was at 70°; not on the right trajectory for us to catch him. I believed him to be a Ju 88 and I felt disappointed that we had no contact. Once back at base I had hardly any sleep as more scrambles followed. I lay wide awake in that awful dispersal and finally dropped off as morning was breaking. I slept until tea time and felt thoroughly washed out.

A few nights afterwards I was scrambled again after a homing flying Hun. We had not much hope of catching it in the Mk IV Beaufighter, but I suddenly got a good visual below me, only to lose him again as the moon disappeared under a dark patch of cumulus cloud. Again, he was at 30° to us, so there was not much hope. We felt frustrated at these fleeting encounters. On 27 February 1943, I was fourth off after having done a forty-minute NFT that afternoon. We had been told that there was a big convoy coming through in the night travelling East, which would reach Bone by dawn. I was airborne on operational convoy patrol for nearly four hours and then later in the night another three hours. I returned to 'St George' after the early morning's work, crashed into bed and slept solidly until 6.30 in the evening. I felt awful when I woke and thanked God I was not on again that night. And all this for no result.

There were often attacks on Algiers, the enemy coming in low to drop his bombs. On 2nd March, I was on duty that evening but well down the list. Suddenly another air raid began. The ack-ack from the Bofors guns was making a hell of a racket but that was nothing to the explosion which shook the building to its foundations. A bomb had landed just outside, narrowly missing Dispersal. As we called it at the time, 'a shaky do!' I went to sleep (or tried to) in my Mae West after that, but there were no more scrambles.

These bouts of intense activity were interspersed with fun and relaxation. One evening Don Munn (Flt Lt DFM) taught us to play bridge: myself, Ian, and Stanley Duff. Don hadn't much patience with us, I'm afraid; he took it quite seriously, and we probably messed about a bit at first, but I progressed quite well and began to get quite good at it over time. In the end bridge became a staple form of entertainment for us and gave us hours of enjoyment.

I often wrote and received letters. The Baxter family in Canada still kept in touch and the Partingtons from Bolton, among others. From time to time I was called upon to censor mail. At other times we would laze around sunbathing on the balcony of St George, or go to the cinema on the American camp. On my first visit there I was made very welcome and met some of their ground officers, Lieutenants John Callahan, Calvin Josslyn and Johnny Moeller, who drove me back to the hotel in their jeep. They stopped and had a drink in the Mess. We quickly became close friends. They would loan me their jeep in exchange for my monthly ration of spirits. This was a fine arrangement for me as I was more of a beer drinker. Quite a lot of my spare time was taken up with visits to Algiers just a few miles away from the 'drome, where I found food and drink of all kinds, cafe's, restaurants, clubs, and cinemas. I was suffering from sweat rash a lot and I found the Turkish baths there were a great improvement on using the camp-kit bath. I usually went into town with colleagues, particularly Joe Berry and Ian Watson, but there were plenty of friendly people around to meet up with. Johnny Callahan introduced me to his crowd. As well as the jeep he had a Citroen and we would all cram into it and go to the pictures. I saw 'Fantasia' twice in this way. On one occasion Johnny, Joss and I were caught in a raid while in the Red Cross Cinema. We stayed inside until the racket was over. Shrapnel was falling on the roof all the time from the terrific barrage put up by the balloons. A few bombs were dropped but no damage was done. On another day Johnny Callahan stopped to lunch, then afterwards I took him up with us on an NFT in Beau 'F'. He enjoyed the trip very much but I was very gentle with him. Joss came with us another time, and in April we had Johnny Moeller. This time it became an operational patrol as news came in of a suspected Hun in the vicinity. We gave chase, but saw nothing. Johnny got more than he had bargained for when he climbed in, but obviously enjoyed himself. Johnny and Joss often came over to play bridge with us and it was a very friendly affair. Ian decided to amuse himself one night by making a pair of slippers out of leather, making comments and asides as we played. Altogether I was having a very sociable time.

As the weeks and months sped by, the Squadron started to suffer some losses. Flt Off. Robinson and his RO, Plt Off. Legrand were reported missing in early March, while searching for a lost Hurricane pilot. Later some wreckage was found on the water and it was supposed that an engine failure low down had caused a crash. Flt Off. Jackson and Plt Off. Bryant were shockingly killed in a terrible smash when their engine cut out on take-off. I had a shaky do myself on March 15th when we scrambled just before dawn in terrible weather conditions to try to spot a bandit approaching low, but with the with cloud base down to 200 feet, we only just managed to get down and land before it damped. We were airborne thirty minutes too long. Williamson chased a 'Recco' job one morning and claimed it as damaged. He was at 20,000 feet and three of his cannons jammed. Hard times!

At the end of March, I was delighted to be made a Flying Officer, backdated to December 1942. Apart from anything else, the money increase was greatly welcomed. In April I was given a 'rest', so the CO asked me to supervise the erecting of a tented site at Setif, where the Squadron would be sending a detachment. Ralph Gibbons and I set off with eight other NCO airmen in the midday sun on 8th April 1943 in three-ton trucks, one of which I drove myself. It was dusk when we reached Bouira, half way, so we stopped the night in a hotel, which fed us wonderfully, and we kicked off again early in the morning, arriving in Setif about four in the afternoon. There were no problems in erecting the camp, and Ralph and I were able to visit our old haunts. On 16th April Flg Off. Ken Rayment landed, as fog had closed in back at Algiers. He told us that Joe Berry and Ian Watson had had to bale out the night before over Algiers. 'Apparently Joe's starboard engine caught fire.'

'Are they OK?' I asked anxiously.

'Joe's fine, but Ian went in the drink. They're searching for him.' We heard next day that Ian had been picked up in a dinghy, but only after the poor chap had spent over six hours on the sea. Joe must have been very relieved to hear Ian was safe, remembering the last time, when his gunner Ted Williams died in the water.

Lt Johnny Callaghan and either Lt Calvin Josselyn or Lt Johnny Moeller, American ground crew with whom Bryan Wild became close friends during his time at Maison Blanche. Bryan had the use of their jeep in exchange for his spirits ration.

9 April 1943, crew of 153 Sqn *en route* to Setif to erect a tented site for the new detachment. Bryan Wild's diary reads, "Awoke early and kicked off for Setif. Had a roadside breakfast a little later..." Ralph Gibbons is third from the right.

There were quite a few Squadron successes around this time. Sqn Ldr Horne, attached to us from 600 Squadron on the Mk VII Beaufighter, shot down a Ju 88 near Algiers. The crew were picked up later in a dinghy. Flt Off. Stephenson, with RO Flt Off. Hall, shot down a Ju 88 near Bone. Flt Off. Mcllenish got two Huns over Algiers, and Flt Sgt Linklater got one destroyed and one damaged at the same time. Flt Lt Duff got a 'probable' over Bone. But these were nothing to Flt Sgt Downing, attached to 600 Squadron, who accomplished a record 'kill' for one sortie. He 'ran across' 5 Ju 52's early in the morning near Bizerta and shot the lot down in fifteen minutes. Ju 52's are slow troop or ammunition aeroplanes and were probably flying in to supply Rommel's beleaguered troops in Tunisia.

Very early on the morning of May 4th 1943, I had just come off night duty at the dispersal hut, when there was a phone call put through to me. It was the CO, who asked if I would mind flying a VIP up to Setif immediately. When I asked who it was, I was astonished to hear that it was none other than one of the great legendary figures of the RAF, Group Captain 'Batchy' Atcherley, now Commanding Officer of the North African night-fighter wing. Every airman at that time would know that this pilot was famous before the war for his dare-devil flying on biplanes at air displays. In the late 1920s he broke the world air speed record, at something around 332 mph. He even flew in formation aerobatics with the wings joined to the other aircraft by ropes.

At 7.15 sharp the great man arrived at the flight hut. He gave Ralph and I a warm smile, and then stood in the well behind me in Beaufighter C8694 for the whole forty-five-minute trip to Setif. Quite naturally I felt a little bit nervous. The weather was a bit dodgy, with thick cloud most of the way and the Atlas Mountains just below. Atcherley chatted to me most of the time. Approaching Setif, I made a gradual descent through quite a bit of cloud to find myself dead on track, thanks to Ralph's excellent navigation. Setif was a grass aerodrome: would this landing be reasonable, or would it be a bit rough like the grass below? To my relief it was a beauty and my passenger praised me for it. It made my day. The Group Captain said a few words with us both, shook hands, waved to us and then strode off, leaving us to fly back to Algiers feeling rather pleased with ourselves.

A few days after this, on May 8th, the Squadron held a dance at the Mess. Officers from the American squadron were there, plus nurses galore from the local military hospital. The Americans provided the dance band and the evening was a huge success. Afterwards, a group of us went with the nurses to escort them back to their hospital up in the mountains near Algiers. We set off well after midnight in a large American ammunition carrier, a kind of jeep, driven by an American GI. We were a merry party, laughing as we were thrown around a bit because of the winding roads. It all went wrong when the GI misjudged a bend and the truck shot off the road and overturned in a ditch, then plunged nose-first down a ravine, finally coming to rest upside down. We were fortunate that the truck didn't catch fire, but most of the occupants had injuries, though not life threatening. I was the only one who was completely unscathed, and so I set off to find help. I eventually found a small police station and managed, just about, to make my French understood. It took some time for the ambulance and rescue teams to put in an appearance. Thankfully no one was very seriously hurt and everyone agreed that it could have been far worse.

On my free days, I would often call at the 144 Maintenance Unit (MU) at the 'drome to see if there were any aircraft they wanted testing. On May 13th, I tested a Hurricane 11C No. HW755 and a Spitfire Vb No. ER500. On 28th May this MU asked for a pilot to test one of their Bristol Bisleys, No. BB150, so I volunteered, and went up with Ralph Gibbons and two passengers. The Bisley was a variant of the Blenheim light bomber designed for ground attack and had been used in Operation Torch, but it was slow and had taken heavy casualties, and had in effect been phased out. I had never piloted one before, but because it belonged to the same family as the Blenheim, Beaufort and Beaufighter, I found this solo flight easy and really enjoyed the trip.

With a few others, Ralph and I were still flying the Mark IV Beaufighters on operations, and the difference between these and the faster Mark VII was very evident to us.[2] To all the airmen, the Mark VII was 'the gen'. For example, on 13 May 1943 there was a raid on Algiers and we scambled in 'O' with Flt Sgt Woods, also in a Mk IV, while Flt Lt Duff and Flg Off. West scrambled in a Mk VII. There was a terrific barrage from the ground and the sky was filled with sparks flying from Algiers' ack-ack. The Huns came in low, so the IV's freelanced. There was no joy for the IVs, but Duffy got a probable. Return fire from the Hun damaged Duffy's engine, but he made it back safely. On other occasions, Ken Rayment shot down two Ju 88s over Bone, and Flg Off. Benn shot down two Ju 88s, both in Mark VIIs. This was good going, and we were glad the Squadron was making some impact, but we wished we could be upgraded soon. On May 22nd I took out a Mk VII Beau with Flg Off. Paghis in the well as instructor and Ralph Gibbons in the back so that he could get experience on this aircraft. On the same night Flg Off. Williamson in his Mk VII shot down two Italian Savoia-Marchetti SM 79s (three-engined medium-sized bombers), and by the end of another two days, the Squadron had claimed one Heinkel III, three Ju 88s, and one SM 79, almost all of these kills being from the Mk VIIs. Ken Rayment's total had been brought to an amazing five destroyed and one damaged. Unsurprisingly, he was awarded the DFC for this remarkable feat.

Sgt Ralph Gibbons in North Africa.

In May 1943 Bryan Wild volunteered to test-fly this Bisley, no BB150, for 144 Maintenance Unit, flying with Ralph Gibbons and two passengers.

On May 24th, the whole squadron moved into extensive tented quarters situated on the coast at Surcouf, near Algiers. This was the large beach made famous the previous year when the American 1st Army successfully invaded Algeria here in Operation Torch. Several wrecked landing craft still littered the shore. The tents were on the grassy headland slightly inland of the beach itself, which was ideal for swimming. I didn't get to enjoy it for too long. On June 5th, I fell ill with a terrible dose of the 'squitters' (diarrhoea) and by the next day I had a high temperature. The Squadron 'Doc' diagnosed a mild dose of dysentery and ordered me to the tented field hospital at Maison Caree, where I was taken by ambulance on Monday 7th and stayed for a week.

During the month of June and early July the Squadron was involved in intense scrambles and patrol duties. The coastal bases, particularly Taher and Bone, were used extensively, allowing the Beaus to spread out along the Med to be on immediate night call. On several occasions, Ralph and I were close to getting enemy contact on the radar, but could never get close enough to produce a positive result. Sometimes there was no sign of the enemy. On one sortie on May 19th, four Beaus, led by Sqn Ldr Munn, with myself, Flt Off. Barker, and Flt Sgt Woods, made a dusk and night sweep of the Western Mediterranean 160 miles north of Algiers, near Majorca and the other Isles, then a long east-to-west low-level flight. The total flying time was 2 hours dusk, 2 hours night. Ralph and I greatly enjoyed the trip, but unfortunately, we didn't spot anything suspicious.

And then, on July 10th came a surprising piece of news. Ralph and I were posted to Egypt to join another Beaufighter Squadron, No 46. This was at a sand aerodrome, Idku, near Alexandria, a Squadron that had supported the land exploits of the 8th Army. I wondered if our posting out of this war zone had anything to do with the 'state of the game' at that point in time. The German desert army was now defeated. The Americans from the west, and the British 8th Army from the east, had squeezed the Nazis out of North Africa to Sicily and Italy. Only the sea patrols still continued as far as operational sorties were concerned.

7

Beaufighters and the Brandy Squadron

While the balance of the war in North Africa swung in the Allies' favour during the early months of 1943, the Allied commanders were debating their next move. Should they follow up in the Mediterranean, creating a network of secure Allied bases from which to dominate the Mediterranean? Or should the Allies work towards cross-Channel invasion of northern France? Britain was heavily committed in the Middle East, and Churchill believed that capture of the Dodecanese Islands— a string of fourteen Islands in the south-eastern Aegean, close to the Turkish Coast, including Rhodes, Kos and Leros—was worth attempting in order to keep up pressure on Germany in the region, provide a secure base for possible activity in the Balkans and Greece and hopefully inspire the neutral Turks to declare against Germany. The main problem was the lack of air cover from remote bases: only the Beaufighter had the necessary range for the RAF, and US Lightnings were the ideal companion for the campaign. Without long-term US back-up, however, embarking on the Dodecanese campaign would be a high-risk strategy. Eisenhower felt that such a campaign, with the huge resources it would require, would delay the war, and he also had the Pacific war with Burma very much in mind. Inevitably, compromises were reached, and the entirety of American air and naval resources necessary for securing the Dodecanese were not forthcoming.

Having now set May 1944 for the D-Day invasion of Normandy, in July 1943, the Allies launched an assault on Sicily, as a springboard for mainland Italy. That month, Mussolini was ousted and a non-Fascist cabinet took over, leading to Italy's surrender to the Allies at the beginning of September. This was a cause for celebration, but Germany wasted no time in moving to secure the Italian-held parts of the Dodecanese Islands from her erstwhile Italian allies. The British had made emergency plans to be put into effect should Italy collapse, and they now scrambled to counteract this move, particularly in Rhodes, Kos and Leros, hoping that German resources might be tied up with the offensive in Italy. But by early September Crete was already in German hands and Britain proved unable to secure Rhodes. With the help of US Lightnings British troops were landed on Kos and Leros in mid-September, joining the wavering Italians already on the ground. The Lightnings were then withdrawn for operations over Italy. By the 19th, Germany already occupied ten other Aegean Islands. The odds were stacked in Germany's favour.

46 Squadron pilots had taken part in the defence of Malta, and reformed as a night-fighter Squadron in 1942. By July 1943 the Squadron, equipped with Beaufighters, had joined 219 (Fighter) Group, commanded by Grp Capt. The Hon. Max Aitken DSO, DFC. This was one of four newly-formed groups operating with 201 (Naval Co-operation) Group, which included 227 and 252 Beaufighter Squadrons. Their overall aim was to contain the Axis forces' movements in the Mediterranean, North Africa, and the Dodecanese Islands.

July 1943, 46 Sqdn, Idku, Alexandria, Egypt

On July 12th 1943, Ralph and I found ourselves as passengers aboard a Dakota FD 832 bound for Egypt and 46 Squadron. The evening before, we had said our farewells to our friends, particularly Joe Berry and Ian Watson.

Idku was a sand aerodrome with no runways, situated a few miles from Alexandria on the Delta coast. The main buildings were Nissen huts. Sleeping quarters for all ranks were tented sites. A circular pit about three feet deep with side walls supported by sand bags, and a bell tent positioned on top of the wall, was 'home' for two to share. Mosquito nets covered the camp beds. Nearby swamps were breeding grounds for 'mossies'; and we always had to wear suede-leather boots as protection from them.

Ralph and I received a warm welcome from the CO, Canadian Wg Cdr Reid, and New Zealander Flt Lt Owen Hooker, the Flight Commander, six foot tall and impressively built. Immediately, we were placed on the 'State of Readiness'; mainly patrols at sea to cover convoys. Other night flights were the usually exercises. There was very little contact with enemy aircraft at this time, now that the North African war zones had been cleared of the Italian and German armies. However, the enemy still controlled many aerodromes in Southern Europe; France, Italy, Greece, Crete and Rhodes, among others, and it was from these that continuous attacks were being made on our shipping. The tiny Island of Malta, now in Allied hands, was in the thick of this activity.

From the moment of our first arrival I sensed that the crews and other officers here were imbued with 'the Spirit of 46': a marvellous feeling of belonging to an important unit, which I had never experienced before. There certainly wasn't this special quality with 153 Squadron. In a matter of a weeks, I knew that the aircrew here were the friendliest I had ever come across. I immediately felt as though I had been there for years. Good humour abounded. The week I arrived there was a Squadron sports day which people talked and laughed about for a long time afterwards. Wg Cdr Reid was an excellent leader, a good sportsman with a dry humour and a ready smile; a clever man and a great organiser who was held in huge affection and respect. I gathered he had been instrumental from the start in establishing and building up 46 Squadron in Idku. I saw that his warm and purposeful personality was a positive influence very much evident in the way things were here. I made many friends in 46, but some were very close indeed. Flt Lt Alistair "Doc" Macdonald was thirty-three years old, and almost a father figure to me, much as Ack Greenwood had been. He quickly dubbed me 'Oscar', because my surname was Wild. Flt Lt Owen Hooker and Flt Off. Jack Barnes were great characters; great fun to be with, and I looked up to them as well. Everyone worked hard but also seemed to be having a good time. On nights off duty, evenings spent in the mess were devoted to card games like Bridge, Pontoon and Poker. Alternatives were chess, and Lie Dice, which I was taught from the beginning here and enjoyed immensely: a marvellous game. There was always someone who could play the piano. The Doc was particularly musical and played the piano, banjo and the ukulele, so he was the focus for plenty of singing sessions in the Mess. But the main off-duty highlights were the trips to Alexandria to visit various hotels, clubs, restaurants, cafés and the cinema, trips usually made by everyone piling into one of the station ambulances driven by Doc Macdonald, the 'patients' being the likes of Sqn Ldr Tommy Scade, Owen Hooker, Jack Barnes and Harry Doodson; or sometimes the CO would lend the Doc his car. We often visited Pastroudis, the cream tea house, famous for its cream pastries, the like of which I had never before tasted. Other favourites were Maxim's Bar, the Officers Union Club, the Sports Club for tennis and swimming, the Montseigneur Restaurant, and Smokey Joe's Café.

One night towards the end of August I was astounded and delighted to see Flt Off. Rhys "Charlie" Peace in town, one of the boys from my 256 Squadron days. I say 'boys', though Charlie himself was in his later thirties. He told me he had come out with 252 Squadron and was now being attached to 46 for a while, which I was very pleased to hear. Over some drinks at the Union Club he told me all the news on 256. It was a great evening, catching up through Charlie. There was a detachment of 256 in Sicily, on Mosquitos, he told me. 'Ian Allan is now Squadron Leader,' he said, waving his cigarette holder in the air with one hand and twirling his handlebar moustache in the other.

'Ian Allan? He was my instructor on Tiger Moths,' I said.

'Maybe so, but luckily he survived that. Well, he's now on night Mosquitos, and has the DSO for getting five Ju 88s in one night sortie over Sicily.'

Officers' Mess, Idku 1943, scene of many happy hours.

Life in Alexandria during this period of the war was comfortable in many respects. Swimming at the Sports Club was a popular pastime.

Aircrew at the Sports Club: From right: Bryan Wild, Owen Hooker, ?Doc MacDonald, and two unknowns.

'Good show!' I said, in amazement.

'His total bag is 14, so he will probably get the DFC next. So tell, me, what's the gen on 46?'

'It's the best squadron I've ever been in. Exceptional. Great bunch of chaps and you'll really enjoy yourself. But I tell you what, Charlie, I'm getting cheesed off with this no flying racket. I report to flight each morning, but there's nothing doing. Still, if it's going to be quiet, this squadron is the best place to do nothing in. Let's just hope it picks up soon.'

'Amen to that,' he said. 'The sooner we can get the job done and all go home, the better.' We stared at our beer for a moment.

He tapped me on the arm, and asked conspiratorially, 'What's this thing about 46 and the brandy?'

'Oh, that!' I laughed. 'Well, this squadron was officially designated the 46 (Uganda) Squadron, but eventually 'Uganda' was replaced with the word 'Brandy', because someone discovered a rather superb immature brandy readily available on Cyprus. It's wonderful stuff: a rich golden yellow; lots of it and cheap. So they started ferrying barrels of the stuff over in the

Beaufighters for the Mess. 'Doc' told me that Flt Lt Dudley ('Let's all have too much to drink tonight') Arundel pancaked back at Idku one night and fell flat on his face as soon as he stepped out of the Beau. Some of the brandy had obviously been reduced on the way over from Cyprus.'

'Ha ha,' said Charlie. 'I see I'm going to like it here.'

During these months good news seemed to be pouring in. The U-Boats in the Atlantic were being swept away. Allied troops were landing in Sicily and Italy. The Russians had launched an offensive on the German invaders. The Americans were hitting back at the Japanese. And there was a combined air offensive by the Americans and British against Germany. During August and September there had been a definite lull in the night-fighter duties of the Squadron. There were sea patrols, as usual, but no missions against the Luftwaffe at that stage. However, the CO mentioned that intruder raids by the Beaus on aerodromes on the other side of the Mediterranean were in the pipeline. One important and worrying event taking place at this time was the invasion by German landing craft of several islands just off the coast of neutral Turkey. Some of these islands had units of British army and navy personnel there, and to counter this threat, long-range aircraft were desperately needed to give cover to these forces, and to support British counter-attack on German landings. Spitfires and Hurricanes didn't have the range for this: the only aeroplane to fit the bill was the Beaufighter. So, out of the blue, as an emergency measure, a section of the Squadron was asked to become a coastal command until further notice. This involved certain important changes to the machine and its crew. First of all the plane was fitted out with bomb rails under each wing to house two 250 lb bombs. Part of the RO's Perspex cupola was cut away to house a machine gun pointing to the rear, a Vickers .303-inch, gas operated. This called upon the radar operator to act as a gunner.

The CO, not satisfied with having the ineffective Vickers gas operated (VGO) gun, decided to experiment with the more powerful .5 inch machine gun used by the Americans in their bombers; so he detailed me to fly to a US base, Devesueir on the banks of the River Nile in southern Egypt, to collect one. I had to stay the night, and the following morning I was sitting alone in the officers' mess having my breakfast when a party of people came in and settled at a nearby table. I quickly realised that one of them was none other than the famous Hollywood star and comedian, Jack Benny, accompanied by another familiar star, Anna Lee. 'Hi there!' he called, 'Come over and join us.' It gave me something to tell the boys on my return.

Back at base, on Sept 2nd 1943, I had a somewhat narrow escape, when, on take-off from Idku with Flt Sgt Gibbons, the starboard engine of Beau V8766 cut out when I was only at a height of 800 feet. I managed

Beaufighters of 46 Squadrons were converted to Coastal Command in the late summer of 1943, to combat the growing German threat to shipping in the Mediterranean. Note the Vickers .303-inch machine gun for the radar operator. Bomb rails were also fitted under each wing to house two 250-lb bombs.

to level out, but I was now heading out to sea. Calling on the RT for the aerodrome to be kept clear, I turned to port on a reciprocal course to base. It was important to turn to port: to complete a single-engined landing the remaining operative engine must always be on the inside of any turn—a drill all pilots learn from the word Go. Although I was now down to a low level on the circuit, I made a successful landing. The 'prop' had stopped completely on the way in. The sleeve valve had gone for a burton.

The next day was 3rd September and we had a 45-minute church parade in the cinema to mark the fourth anniversary of the outbreak of war. That evening we heard the great news that the 8th Army had crossed from Sicily to Calabria, in southern Italy. It was an eventful week all round for me, but not at all in the way I wanted. For a number of weeks, Ralph had not been himself, seeming moody. Now he went down with sandfly fever on 7th September and was taken to sick quarters, and I also felt rough with the 'squitters'. That evening we were given a late flash: the Squadron was on twenty-four hours' notice to move, but we didn't know where. The next day the mess cheered the wonderful news that Italy had surrendered, and we were all buzzing with excitement. Was the Squadron moving to Italy? Between the excitement and feeling ill, I was very restless that night and hardly slept. In the morning the Doc had no hesitation in diagnosing scabies. I was moved by ambulance to the 8th General Hospital in Alexandria where I was introduced into a quiet ward with three other chaps, one naval and two army officers. I was given hot baths and smothered in sulphur ointment for almost a week, which was not very pleasant, but I managed to spend most of the days playing chess with my new naval friend. The food was not too bad, though there was not enough of it, but I thought the nurses were grand. I tried not to be too impatient at being there. On the Saturday night I was allowed to go to the English girls' school across the way to hear the singer Josephine Baker give us a small turn. She wasn't too spectacular. Still, I felt it was good of her to come.

When I arrived back on Monday September 13th, there was a surprising visitor to the Squadron: Group Captain Max Aitken, Lord Beaverbrook's son. As the Wing's Commanding Officer, he came to inform the CO that a section of 46 would be sent to Cyprus on Detachment, to deal with the invasion of the Islands of Cos and Leros by the Germans. About half the squadron had already moved to Lakatamia aerodrome, near Nicosia, Cyprus, and some Beaus had been converted for coastal command. Over the next few days, crews left for Cyprus one by one. Ralph was still ill, having been moved to hospital in Alexandria the day I came out, so I was left kicking my heels at Idku with the other tail-enders, all of us frustrated at the lack of operational activity. A great deal of our time was spent in 'killing it': visits to Alexandria to the usual haunts, or swimming at Abu Queir, a small beach resort near Alex. Charlie Peace had acquired a Dachshund, left behind by the retreating Germans, which he named Fritz. Fritz was good company, and I often took him with me on these swimming expeditions. I still kept my diary going, but quite often I had virtually nothing to enter, except how much I had won or lost at bridge, and which dreadful film I had been to see. I haunted the Orderly Officer's lair, hoping to hear that I would be moving to Cyprus at any time, but I had to wait for Ralph, who was still stuck in hospital. By 19th there were only six crews left in Idku. In the world outside we heard of huge changes. The Italian fleet had formed into Valetta, Malta, with battleships, submarines, cruisers and destroyers, and later the fleet moved into Alexandria itself. I had not flown for a fortnight when on 21st I was airborne at 0630 for 30 minutes in Beau 'T' for 135 MU at 'Kilo 40'. I was told that my coastal Beau was not ready because there was some trouble with the port engine, so I hung around until 1145 when I was given a new 'Beau' to get me back to Ikdu. I visited the hospital in the afternoon, looking in on 'Chico' Bower, who was in with shrapnel wounds, and Ralph, of course. I learned, to my dismay (and his, no doubt), he would be another five days yet, so to cheer myself up I went to the Union Club and had a 'session' with Jack Cockburn and Bob Peasley.

Better news came in the morning when I was told that the aircraft I brought from 153 MU had been allotted to me, though I would be sharing it with Plt Off. Jackson. I tried not to chafe too much at the next five days. I cleaned the kite (letter 'P'), and longed to fly it, but it turned out not to be

46 Squadron was Bryan Wild's favourite posting, with a great spirit of camaraderie. Messing about at Ikdu are: left to right: Bryan Wild, ?, Doc MacDonald, Sherriff Muir, Charlie Peace (upside down), unknown bending, Jack Barnes, back.

ready. It had a 'mag' drop on the starboard engine and was in maintenance quite a while. I wondered how long I would keep it after all. Finally on the morning of September 27th, Flt Sgt Jackson kicked off in it for Nicosia with about seven other crews, and I watched them disappear with a sigh. Charlie Peace, Rex Archer, Flt Lt Muir, who we called 'Sheriff', and the Doc were still here, with Dave Crerar and a few others. We just had to make the best of it. The aerodrome itself was busy. 89 Squadron were here in force, and four crews of 108 (Malta) Squadron were also here, so there was plenty of coming and going, and plenty of people to socialise with. I was invited out with Wg Cdr Kain to the Officer's Mess at Abu Queir, with Dave Crerar, Rex Archer, Charlie Peace and George Webb of 89 Squadron. George told us they were shortly to be going to India. He seemed excited about it. I tried to put my own frustration to one side and settle into the routine.

On 29th Ralph came out of hospital at last, quite fit now, and my hopes rose, but it made no difference; we were still not transferred. Ralph's mood didn't seem to have lifted and because we weren't flying I didn't see much of him.

On Saturday 2nd October, Owen Hooker landed back at Idku from Nicosia. I began to feel that things were looking up and that evening we resumed our bridge sessions. On the same day I talked with Ralph about our own situation. We didn't seem to be getting on too well, and the inactivity didn't help. The outcome was that I sat down and wrote a letter to the CO first thing in the morning, asking permission for a RO swap with 153 Squadron. My old friend Deryk Hollinrake, with whom I got on so well during my Squires Gate days, was now nearby with 153 as a radio operator, and I asked to be teamed up with him if possible. Nothing came of it: as it fell out, the wider events of that day overtook such minor matters. After I had written and sent my letter to the CO, Owen, Dave, Rex and I went into Alex. We had lunch at the Union Club and finally spent the evening there playing snooker, after a memorably glorious meal at Maxims. Too well-fed and happy to bother trekking back to base, the four of us decided to live it up and stay the night at the Leroy Hotel. A perfect day.

A perfect day. But the next morning on return to camp, our warm feelings evaporated when we walked into the Mess. It was immediately evident to us that something was very wrong. We were told the grave news that four crews were missing from operations the day before. Our hugely popular CO, Wing Commander George Reid and Fg Off. Bob Peasley, was one. The others were: Sqn Ldr Bill Cuddie (Flight Commander) with Flg Off. Leonard Coote; WO Edward 'Sludge' Ledwidge with Sgt John Rowley; and WO Les Holmes with Flt Sgt Mark Bell. 89 Squadron also had two casualties. Such a long list. We sat down in some shock and listened to the few details that were known. We knew that the Island of Cos just off the Turkish Coast was manned by a small garrison of British troops after its acquisition from the enemy in mid-September: Bill Cuddie had piloted the first Allied aircraft to land there on 14th of that month and 46 Squadron had operated since then to assist in establishing the garrison, providing convoy cover and offensive patrol over the island and carrying special equipment in. The Germans were now mounting a counter-offensive using landing craft with air support above to land their troops on the Island. Our Beaus were the only long-range fighters in the area that could reach the islands in the archipelagos: the reason why we had been converted to coastal command. Our crews had come in very low over the sea on their approach to Cos, strafing the landing crafts, but had been attacked by the German single-engined Messerschmitt 109s which were escorting Heinkel III bombers. This was all the information we had for now. The full news only trickled in slowly over the coming days, and in the meantime we lived with anxious uncertainty. The evening of the next day brought the news that Sqn Ldr Cuddie had been seen to go down in flames and was definitely lost, together with his RO, Plt Off. Coote. WO's Holmes and Ledwidge, with their navigators, had both force-landed safely in Turkey. News about the CO was still very vague, but there were hopes that he might be safe. What was certain was that a strong force of Germans had landed successfully on Cos. The next day, 6 October 1943, two of our North American pilots, Jim 'Tex' Holland and Joseph 'Arthur' Horsfall came back from the detachment. Art told us that there had been several sorties that Sunday. He himself and Roger Colley, his RO, had been scrambled first just after 0400 hours, with Sqn Ldr Scade, Fg Off. Atkins, and WO Boswell, on a shipping strike against ships invading Cos. When they arrived they could see German vessels attacking the Island and went in and bombed and strafed them. Art and the others got back to Lakatamia safely at 0845 hours. The CO and his RO Bob Peasley had operated from Idku; Tex and Art knew no more than we did about what might have happened to them. Tex had scrambled later the same morning, with three aircraft from 227 Squadron. They had tangled with some Ju 87s off Cos and in the ensuing dogfight shot down three of them. Tex said he had come back with 'three-quarters of a Stuka out of the do'. He had claimed one shared and another damaged.

By Thursday 7 October 1943, Cos was occupied by the enemy, and our hopes waned of hearing better news of George Reid. This incident overshadowed us, dominating our thoughts relentlessly, and we chafed even more, if that were possible, at our inactivity, but we set ourselves to carry on with our Squadron life as well as we could. Owen and I played a lot of bridge with some of the boys from 89 Squadron. We saw films like 'Snow White and the Seven Dwarfs' and 'Beyond the blue Horizon', starring Dorothy Lamour, at the Station Cinema. The usual swimming at Abu Queir took place. Then on the Friday I was told I was going to Cyprus the next day with Ralph Gibbons, to join the depleted detachment. At last! We tested Beaufighter 'D' for 45 minutes in the afternoon and in a fit of high spirits at the thought of more imminent action I beat up the Mess before landing. Unfortunately, the Station CO was in to tea, so I had to report to his office the next morning. There was an ENSA show on at the station camp that night, but I was not in the mood, and spent the evening in the Mess playing bridge with Owen, until the ENSA party invaded the Mess after the show for the cold buffet we had laid on for them, and I went to bed more cheerily than I had felt earlier in the evening.

The station CO was lenient. In the morning, Saturday 9 October 1943, after a very mild ticking off for the beat-up, I was quickly dismissed and at last kicked off for Cyprus with Ralph, after much panic to get our kit together. The kite was packed to the gunnels with kit bags and general supplies, not to mention Alf Tate, the Officers' Mess cook, who managed to squeeze in somehow. We landed at Latakamia at 1320. This aerodrome was situated just 5 miles south of Nicosia, the capital in the centre of the island, on a flat plain which runs roughly east to west right across the territory, with ranges of mountains to the north and to the south. The whole complex at Lakatamia was a tented outfit. I was very pleased to find I was to share a tent with Arthur Horsfall. He was a likeable chap, open and friendly, with a confident, happy manner that made him easy to get along with. He was only couple of months younger than me, and was extremely fit and strong, having been brought up, so he told me, in the beautiful mountainous region of Jasper in Alberta, Canada, with skiing in the winter and hiking in the summer. He had been at University before he joined up, studying engineering, and had worked as a tour guide in Jasper Park as a summer job. He looked the picture of outdoor living, with sun-lightened brown hair and blue eyes. He was interested to hear about my stay in Moose Jaw and my subsequent 'tour' of Eastern Canada. He laughed when I told him hesitantly about our less-than-enthusiastic impressions of Montreal and Toronto. 'You've hardly seen Canada at all,' he said. 'When the war's over, you'll have to come out to Alberta and I'll show you the real thing!'

While I was unpacking my things, Arthur told me that bad news had just reached the detachment: Wing Commander Reid had definitely been

Beaufighters at Lakatamia tented site, near Nicosia, Cyprus, October 1943. The 46 Squadron detachment had been established in September as part of the attempted defence of the Dodecanese Islands Cos and Leros from German invasion.

killed. 'I'm sorry I've got such bad news for you when you've just come in,' he said. 'They picked up Bob Peasley out of the water, and he's safe in hospital in Turkey. But he says the CO went down with the kite.'

'It's what we dreaded, then,' I said. 'Do you know any more details?'

Arthur told me that after the first wave of attack that took off at 04.00 from Lakatamia early that Sunday morning, in which he himself had taken part, the CO left Idku at 07.00 with two other aircraft from 89 Squadron. When they reached Cos, the formation attacked the German shipping with cannon and bombs, but came under very fierce fire and all three planes were hit. One of 89's radio observers, Sgt Trevett, was hit in the eye from flak, but he navigated safely back to base even so. I murmured in admiration at this feat. Art nodded and continued. 'Flt Lt Wright from 89 Squadron told us that the three planes had turned away and were heading back to base when they were attacked by six Arado 196s, the German floatplanes. He saw Wing Commander Reid's plane in trouble but wasn't sure what happened to it. But now Bob has been able to tell the story himself. Bob says their plane was hit going very low over the water. They made strikes on some shipping but got hit on the starboard engine and port wing and they were under attack from some Arados. The CO managed to keep her up for a while, but she was difficult to handle; then the starboard engine went up in flames and the port engine overheated, and that was it: they turned, spun and crashed into the sea from about 300 feet. He doesn't remember actually hitting the sea but he came to under the water and struggled to get out—a horrible experience—and his Mae West jacket buoyed him up to the surface and kept him afloat until he was picked up. He was completely alone; there was no sign of George Reid. So now the CO's officially assumed killed.' What a blow to us all! It hit us hard. Such a thoroughly nice man and a great leader. He had a way with him of bringing us together and of making us feel we were part of something special. It really was a huge loss.

'And Sludge?' I asked, after a pause, meaning Edward Ledwidge.

'Better news, I'm glad to say. He's OK. But he confirmed what we heard already about Bill Cuddie. He saw him go down. Sludge was in the third sortie that took off just after midday. Squadron Leader Cuddie was leading, with Ledwidge, Jackson and Holmes. They saw a huge invasion force on the north side of the island. Bill Cuddie said over the intercom, 'Let's have a go at that lot!' so they spread out and went in low to attack at full speed. There was tremendous flak from the ships. Sludge said he saw the Squadron Leader veer off suddenly and then the plane just exploded—went up in a huge ball of flame and black smoke. Ledwidge bombed some shipping but he got hit as well. He thinks the flak hit the petrol tank. He bolted for the Turkish coast trailing fire and smoke, but the fuel leaked out and they had to ditch. The wing just fell off as it hit the water. They were a hell of a time in the sea in the dinghy, paddling like blazes and trying to head for a lighthouse on the Turkish coastline. They made it after about eight hours. Holmes and Bell had to ditch as well; one of their engines was hit. They were picked up by boat. They are in the same hospital as Bob, but I think Ed was moved somewhere else.' Art ran his hand through his hair and shook his head. 'It was a hell of a do. I don't suppose you saw Jackson's plane after he got back? It's a wonder he ever made it. More holes than a sieve.'

'Wasn't there another sortie later on?' I asked.

'Yes, but it didn't come to anything,' said Arthur. 'Only Dudley Arundel went from our Squadron; the other four were from 227. The Germans were ready for them, with smoke screens all along the coastline, and it was impossible to see any shipping clearly. Anyway, the ack-ack was just too hot; the boys had to come home. At least they got back safely.'

It was a parcel of news to absorb. 3rd October became known in the records of 46 Squadron as 'Black Sunday'.

Next evening I had my first taste of Nicosia, a small, pleasant city. My guides were Flt Lt Johnny Atkins, Fg Off. Jack Barnes, and Art Horsfall. It was always warm in Cyprus, and the grateful climate tempted us to linger late into the night. We got a taxi back well after midnight, but when we arrived home, the driver tried to charge us ten shillings, which we considered extortionate. A heated argument ensued until finally Jack Barnes threatened to take his door off, after which a reluctant agreement was reached and we finally paid eight shillings, feeling that honour had been somewhat satisfied.

If I had been grumbling in my diary about having nothing interesting to write, all that now changed. For the rest of the month and into most of November, I experienced the most concentrated operational flights of my entire career as a pilot, and in a rather strange twist of the game it happened to me as a coastal command aviator, not as a night-fighter. I did not put in one hour of night flying during this hectic spell. These missions, continuous for about a month, were all involved in the one objective: to repel the German landings on the Dodecanese islands, mainly Cos and Leros. Apart from our beleaguered troops on the islands, there were two spearheads: the Royal Navy, with a strong flotilla of cruisers and destroyers; and the RAF's Beaufighters. There was always radio contact between these two groups. Earlier in the year, our own Flt Lt 'Sheriff' Muir had pioneered a new type of communication whereby the ship could act as control for the night-fighter. This involved a 'mother' beacon for the controlling ship for air escort work at night, a great innovation, which 46 Squadron had been operating for some months. Many of these sorties were free from combat. They represented hours and hours of patrols over our warships, the Cruisers HMS *Penelope*, HMS *Aurora* and HMS *Pheobe*, each with three or four attendant destroyers. Other sorties brought us in direct contact with the enemy Heinkels and Me 109's. Some were successful, some partly successful; in some we suffered RAF casualties. The formations of aircraft usually consisted of three or four machines and we often flew on joint operations with other Beau squadrons, 227 and 252 mainly, also based at Cyprus. There were 'shipping strike' actions in the vicinity of Rhodes, Cos and Leros, to try and take out the enemy shipping; low-level intruder patrols which were particularly dangerous. I was involved in around fourteen of the various kinds of expeditions. All these took place in daylight, and in some cases in dreadful weather conditions with heavy rain and dramatic thunderstorms.

The weather was certainly one of the *dramatis personae*. I remember clearly having great difficulty one day in locating our warships through thick cloud and thunderstorms and lashing rain, returning home frustrated through gathering dusk in the middle of an electric storm, the lightning making the cloud around us flicker menacingly. Later, when I tried to dry out in the mess with a few beers, Art told me, 'At least you're not completely in the drink like one of the chaps from 227. He ditched in the sea south of Cyprus, but got in a dinghy OK and was rescued.' A few days later again the skies were throwing rain down on Ralph and me even as we sat in the van on the way to our briefing at 15.00 hours with another three crews. By the time we arrived at dispersal we were already soaking wet. With no time to change or get dry before taking off at 16.15 we were all feeling particularly damp and we became further cheesed off at our inability to see anything below us after a fruitless couple of hours' searching through the rain-soaked air. Ralph's voice over the radio said lugubriously, 'Who says it's all sun and blue skies in the Mediterranean?' A few minutes later the Island of Scarponto was spotted to starboard; we knew it had an Italian airbase which was now used by the Luftwaffe. We all bolted, heading home in close formation, lights on, in the gathering dark and the pouring rain. When we were half way home, a break in the cloud surprised us with a view of our lost convoy progressing peacefully across the sea below us. Again a few days after that came another five-hour patrol, taking off after an early breakfast into what seemed like a wall of rain and lightning. It came as a great relief to me when it cleared west of the Island and I no longer had to strain to see outside the cockpit. As on the other three patrols, we had no incident to report on return.

It was different the next day for Tex Holland and his radio operator, Henry Bruck, on an offensive sweep in the evening over Rhodes. They were attacking German shipping with cannon and machine guns under intense ack-ack from the harbour when two Me 109s entered the fray. In the ensuing dog fight, Tex attacked one of the fighters. Tex's Beau was hit by returning fire down the port side and that engine caught fire, smoke pouring out and behind. The Me 109 was nowhere in sight by now but Tex had to bring the Beau down, ditching successfully onto the water. He managed to get back to Henry Bruck in the tower, but he was in a very bad way, shot straight through the chest by a 22-mm cannon shell. Henry died shortly afterwards of his wounds. Tex bobbed about in the dinghy in the dark until a Squadron search located him and directed a launch to pick him up and take him to hospital in Turkey. He didn't make it back to the Squadron until the end of October.

In the middle of it all I flew back for a four-day rest visit in Idku, less than two hours away. It was wonderful to see a lot of 'old' faces once more. On walking into the mess in the morning I was immediately snapped up to play bridge with Owen Hooker, 'Bish' Martin and Johnny Atkins, and that was pretty much how the few days passed, apart from the evening when the whole camp went to see the ENSA show 'Razzle' at the station cinema. It was grand to be back. The second afternoon I was airborne at 16.00 with Plt Off. Cockburn RO, in one of the new Mk VIII Beaus, for an aircraft test, doing single-engined flying with 'props' fully flattened. It was a very nice machine to fly. I enjoyed my break, but was happy to return to Lakatamia on 22nd October and thrilled to discover that Doc MacDonald was to be posted here for a while. In anticipation I tidied up the tent and went into Nicosia with Arthur to buy some things from the Officer's shop there.

Wednesday 27th October 1943 was an eventful day. It started in grand style with a huge explosion early in the morning, literally shaking us awake. It sounded really close by, and seemed to go on and on. Arthur and I staggered outside to see what was happening. All hell was let loose. One of 252 Squadron's Beaufighters had crashed on take off only about 200 yards from our tent. After the initial boom of the impact the ammunition carried on exploding for another hour. Both the airmen got out OK. Thankfully the Beau was a tough aircraft and other crewmen than these two had reason to be thankful for it.

That same afternoon we were briefed at 1400 hours for last light cover naval escort of a cruiser and three destroyers around Castelrosso Island, heading for the Turkish coast. Four of us in the flight, Dudley Arundel (leading), Art Horsfall, Boswell and myself, plus RO's, were airborne at 16.14. I was leading the second section with Boswell as my number two. We found the convoy easily despite the bad weather, but as dusk fell, at 1800 hours, the cruiser in RT touch with us vectored us to a bunch of hostiles approaching from the West at 12,000 feet. Arundel immediately ordered the planes to fly at 13,000 feet. The bunch of hostiles came into view and, to our astonishment, we saw fifteen Ju 88's in a very tight V-shaped formation heading directly to attack the convoy, a frightening sight. The four of us peeled off and attacked them from the beam and from behind. There was heavy return fire but all four Beaus fired their four cannons and six machine guns, causing such havoc among the enemy that they scattered and fled for home at full throttle the way they had come. Flt Lt Arundel and Arthur, the front pair in the attack, claimed aircraft damaged: Arundel two, Horsfall one. In the second wave I thought I may have damaged one, but owing to the confused state of the encounter I didn't claim anything later. The light was very poor with lots of cloud about and I couldn't be definite. We couldn't get close enough to follow up and split the formation: our Beau's were too slow. However, we all felt satisfied that we had driven off a potentially dangerous group of bandits. The return fire from the Ju 88s had been heavy, and it inflicted some damage to two of our Beaufighters. WO Boswell had to return to base on one engine. It turned out that he had been particularly lucky: one bullet passed through the Perspex only one inch from his head. I was lucky not to be hit, but as far as I was concerned, it was the first time I had been fired at by the enemy, and it was quite an experience. We returned to the convoy to find a hostile dropping flares, but he saw us coming and buzzed off.

The next evening I went with the boys into Nicosia for the usual round. On our way out of one of our haunts, the Empire, I found a little kitten shivering in the hallway. It returned my gaze, came over and rubbed against me. It was as thin as a rake. I had had a little too much to drink by that time, which perhaps explains why I brought it back to camp with me inside my jacket. I called it 'Timbaki' after a popular night club singer in Nicosia. It slept at the foot of the bed and in the morning I woke to find the kitten next to my left ear. I gave it some milk, which soon disappeared. I was pleased to be able to stay around the tent to settle him in, and I spent the afternoon filling in, and looking back through, my log book. I thought I might be flying the next day so after a quick snack in the NAAFI I returned early. Arthur answered my questioning look when I got back and gestured to my bed. 'Timbaki is still here,' he said, 'and seems set to stay.'

I did some more convoys over the next few days, some very long and mostly without incident. On one occasion I was airborne at 09.55 as Number 2 to Arthur, and we reached the convoy successfully at 11.00 only to discover that the two Beaus already on the convoy had been vectored on to a low-flying Ju 88, which they eventually shot down. We hung around for five hours but nothing else happened.

One favourite day trip took us to the lovely village of Kyrenia on the coast, with its 12th Century castle. A small lagoon provided marvellous swimming facilities. I took the Ford van with about a dozen chaps on board over the very steep, winding road. I had great difficulty changing gear up the mountain pass and had to put up with a number of jeers and jokes about my driving, but it was worth it for the trip. The journey itself was spectacular, particularly Saint Hilarion Castle at the top of the pass, on its rocky outcrop, with dramatic views all round. Arthur said the country reminded him of home. 'That smell!' he said, breathing it in, 'Pine trees, leaves, clear water!' Once in Kyrenia, Arthur generally liked to swim with the rest, but 'Butch' Charles and I would go sightseeing and have a good look round the castle. On other days we played football. I took my tourist negatives into Nicosia for development and sometimes had a little trouble getting some of them off the censor, but was finally successful. And on the same day that Tex Holland arrived back, 30th October, Flt Lt Bill Kemp from 227 Squadron belly-landed at the 'drome after being shot up by an enemy fighter during a dog fight in which three German aircraft were downed. Bill's aircraft stalled while firing at the enemy, who then blew away Kemp's rudder control hydraulics. As if that wasn't enough, the Vickers gun jammed so his navigator couldn't return fire. They were lucky to get down in one piece. Bill was a strong, likeable character. He was very brave, couldn't care less about rank, and was loyal to his friends. He was well-respected among the boys, and we got on very well with him, as he was great fun to be with. The next day, Bill, Tex, Arthur and I had a trip into Nicosia together. There always seemed to be something happening and I never felt bored. But the best was yet to come, as on 3rd November Jack Barnes and Jenx (Plt Off. Jenkinson) arrived back from Idku bringing the Doc and Dennis Barney with them. They also brought a parcel of great news. WO Ledwidge, now commissioned and back from Turkey, had been posted home, and given the DFC for his part in the 'Black Sunday' operation. Flt Sgt Jackson had been awarded the DFM. Sgt Trevett, the RO from 89 who had navigated safely home after being shot in the eye, got the DFM for this feat. Paul Sage and Jack Cockburn were also going home. Flt Lt Arundel and Flt Lt Owen Hooker were now Squadron Leaders. Sqn Ldr Scade had become Wing Commander and CO 46 Squadron. I was delighted for them all, especially Owen. While the rest of the boys showed the Doc round Nicosia, Dennis Barney, Butch and myself had fried eggs, tomatoes, beans and fried bread in the Mess. Later when everyone came back and joined us, we celebrated the promotions in proper style.

Rhodes now became the centre of the action. On 5th November, we heard the awful news that four out of five Beaufighters of 227 Squadron had been shot down near the Island by four Me 109's. It was my day off,

Wing Commander Tommy Scade (left) and Flt Lt Rossiter, Idku. Tommy Scade became CO 46 Squadron after the death of the much-loved Wing Commander Reid in October 1943.

Flt Lt Bryan Wild, on a day trip to Kyrenia, Cyprus in October.

46 Squadron air crew at either Kyrenia or St Helarion Castle, Cyprus.

Fritz the Dachshund with Bryan Wild (left) and air crew. Rhys Trevor 'Charlie' Peace, wearing his usual shorts, is feeding Fritz, and Timbaki the cat is climbing over Charlie's right shoulder.

Doc MacDonald (left) with unidentified companion at Lakatamia on Cyprus. Note the well-stocked drinks cabinet. Timbaki the cat is on the table, so this may be Bryan Wild's tent.

but Art was stood by to search for their missing crews. In the end Bill Kemp and another from 227 searched without success. As far as I could see, these daylight sweeps around the Greek Islands were suicide missions for our planes. The Beau was no match for a single-engined fighter like a Me 109, and we were operating at our extreme range without enough support from our own single-engine fighters for cover. After hearing this bad news, I had my usual meal in the NAAFI and went to bed early, having been briefed at 18.00 with WO Ron Lindsey for first light cover in the morning to the *Phoebe* cruiser and two destroyers. As I got up at 04.30 for the trip these considerations thrust themself into my mind and my thoughts were sombre. However, the sortie was straightforward, though long and therefore tiring. I was looking forward to a lie-in the next day, Sunday 7th, but it was not to be. At four in the morning another of 252 Squadron's Beaus crashed on take-off and burst into flames shortly after the pilot and observer scrambled out with minor injuries. This was 252 Squadron's second crash close to our tent in a fortnight. 'Do you think they're aiming for us?' asked Arthur. 'Has somebody upset them?'

'Have you been singing again before breakfast?' I asked him. But we were all relieved no one was hurt.

In the afternoon I painted Walt Disney's character, Pluto, on the side of Beaufighter 'P', while Arthur lounged around chatting. We discussed

252 Squadron Beaufighter crashed on take-off near Wild's and Horsfall's tent at Lakatamia, on 7th November; the second such occurrence. Both crews escaped serious injury. Ralph Gibbons at the damaged wing.

the German's new weapon, a radio-controlled 'flying' bomb. Arthur had studied aero-engineering, so was particularly interested. 'It's fired by jet-propulsion from a Dornier Do217,' he told me. 'It has a wing-span of eight feet and it can be put into a controlled dive for the target.'

'Formidable!' I said, 'And it's going to be a heck of a job shooting them down, especially at night. There!' I stood back. 'What do you think?'

'Looks good,' said Arthur. 'Are you going to do any of the others? How about Donald Duck for 'D'?'

'Yes, why not? But not now. Jack Barnes has taken 'B' back to base, and I've been appointed Bar Officer in his place'.

I was looking forward to hosting the bar. It was the centre of Squadron life, and I knew that my new role would cause comment. I enjoyed it all so much that one night I gave Horrocks, the usual bar tender, the night off, and looked after the bar myself. It felt good to be leaning on the bar, looking on with a benevolent eye and listening to the friendly debate on various wide-ranging subjects. Tex, Dave, Doc and Arthur played a game of blackjack. The evening finished up with a fry-up of egg and chips.

Tension in the Squadron was mounting as news of the Germans' activities in the Dodecanese islands became more grave. Over the past few days we had been mounting patrols of two aircraft at night over Leros to try and prevent German aggression towards the Island, but on 11

Beau P ND155 at Lakatamia, Cyprus, November 1943. On the afternoon of 7 November Bryan Wild painted a picture of Pluto onto this aircraft, while Arthur Horsfall looked on.

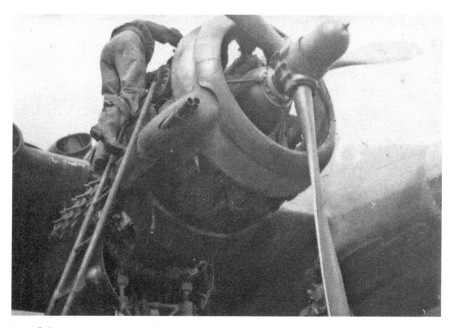

Beaufighter maintenance, Lakatamia, Cyprus, November 1943.

November 1943, the word was that Leros was about to be invaded. As well as eight thousand Italian troops, the Island's forces had now been supplemented by three thousand British. The Germans had retaliated with air bombardments from the end of September onwards, causing casualties and damage on the land and sinking one British destroyer at sea. The situation was deteriorating.

I was down to be first off that night with WO Lindsey second, WO Boswell third and Sqn Ldr Arundel fourth, but now all available crews and aircraft were put on the ready, standing by for maximum effort. In the evening ten crews were briefed for strike if ordered. All the aircraft were being bombed up with 250-pounders. If the strike was cancelled, I would be going on convoy at first light. As it happened, it was my convoy stooge that was cancelled: the invasion of Leros by Germany had started. At 08.45, seven crews comprising Sqn Ldr Arundel, Sqn Ldr Kemp (227 Squadron), Fg Off. Bliss (also 227), WO Boswell, WO Lindsay, Plt Off. Jackson and myself, were briefed at 08.45 for shipping strike off Leros. Our task was especially to bomb landing barges. We were airborne at 09.25 and flew over the Turkish coast in 'Vic' formation through rain showers on the way in. We approached Leros from the North East. It was a shocking sight, the Island already being shelled and dive-bombed by Ju 87s or Stukas, the two-man dive bombers, terrifying to those on the ground. We circled round the north of island only to be fired on by our own 'ack-ack'. I steeled myself as I flew right into the flak, but wasn't hit, thank the Lord. Coming out of it, I saw a convoy of enemy landing barges escorted by destroyers over to the North West and overhead, protecting them, were Me 109's. These fast fighter planes were in a commanding position above us, and to add to the difficulty of the situation we saw seven Ju 88s only about two miles away, also above us. The German forces' formation was tight: we saw no loose ships, so we turned for home at speed, landing hours later still with our bombs on board, and feeling almost unbearable frustration. The exercise had been futile. With such strong air cover, and that above us, there was nothing we could do. I was very much afraid that Leros had had it. At one point I had thought this sortie was going to end for us like the Cos affair, but this time we all landed safely.

There were bags of mail for me on my return, a backlog of letters come home to roost at last. I spent the afternoon of the next day writing five letters and umpteen Christmas cards. Christmas was something to look forward to. It was nice to think we might reach it. Arthur met up with a pal of his in the Mess so I didn't see much of him until the evening, when I came to readiness with Arthur, Ron Lindsey and Sgt Steels, knowing we might be called for first light convoy cover. We finished the evening with a grand fry-up in the mess, with eggs and chips and beans.

The next day was Sunday 14th November 1943, and it turned out to be one of the last missions of the campaign. It was a major strike against German ground troops and landing craft on Leros, and involved two Beau squadrons, 46 and 227, both based at Lakatamia: four aircraft from 46 and eight from 227. The whole show was led by newly-promoted Sqn Ldr Bill Kemp of 227. The four from 46 were: Flt Lt Dave Crerar, leader, with Pilot Officer Charles; Fg Off. Arthur Horsfall with Flt Sgt James 'Roger' Colley; WO Ronald Lindsey with Flt Sgt Alfred Gardner; and myself with Flt Sgt Ralph Gibbons as usual. We were briefed at 10.00 and each aircraft was loaded with two 250lb bombs.

We were airborne at 11.45 on a drab and cloudy day. For some unknown reason three of 227 aircraft turned and headed back to base before the formation had reached the tiny island of Castelrosso. The rest of us continued on flying near to Rhodes to approach the island of Leros from the north east at a height of about 500 feet.

Quite out of the blue a Heinkel III bomber appeared out of cloud and to port of us. The whole formation turned and Crerar and I, who happened to be on that side of the group, peeled off to attack it and got there before the others. Crerar was well ahead of me. Turning in behind the Heinkel, he closed in and fired three bursts with the cannons and machine guns, two on the turn and then one from dead astern. I didn't see any hits on the Heinkel but I could clearly see Dave's cannon shells kicking up in the sea just ahead of it. When Crerar broke off the attack, it was not clear to me whether Dave had hit it or not. At any rate, the Heinkel still kept its course after Dave had turned away. I followed up with maximum speed, firing one sustained burst of cannon fire from dead astern. It was only about five seconds, but I saw my shots go home along the fuselage and a few seconds after that the Heinkel ditched into the sea, right under my nose. I flew over it and headed away. Over Leros my attention was caught by a dark cloud of dust rising slowly from the centre of the Island: it seemed there was heavy bombing in progress. We were then ordered back to base.

But suddenly the whole picture changed as, in one frightening moment, a bunch of six ME 109's appeared at around 3,000 feet as if by magic from the patchy cloud layer to pounce on our formation. It was the classic case

[sequence of eight photographs Heinkel]: 14 November 1943, close to the Island of Leros: an attack on Heinkel 6N+EP of II/KG100 by two Beaufighters from 46 Squadron. Photographs taken with the camera of Beaufighter JL913/E, Flt Lt David Crerar and RO Plt Off. L Charles, whose shots can be seen hitting the right wing and kicking up the water. Flg Off. Bryan Wild with RO Flt Sgt Ralph Gibbons in JK989/S followed up to complete the kill. *Photographs: Crown Copyright, Ministry of Defence*

in aerial combat of the superior single-engined fighters striking down from above onto slower types of fighter aircraft at sea level; the Beaus being no match for the Messerschmitts. There was only one course of action under these circumstances: it was a case of run and sweat it out. Sqn Ldr Kemp on the RT ordered us to scatter and run for coast. I immediately jettisoned the bombs and for the first time ever in a Beaufighter I used the emergency engine booster by pushing the throttle levers through the full scope of the control box. Flying low down at well over 300 miles per hour, I sped for the coast and the Turkish mountains via the low clouds. WO Lindsey was on my left, keeping close. Ralph Gibbons, manning the Vickers gas-operated machine gun in the rear, was firing at a 109 behind us. Suddenly he yelled that another was closing in rapidly and firing at us. My heart started to pound as dead ahead of me in the sea, cannon fire suddenly appeared, kicking up the water into tiny fountains.

We were flying hard, faster than I thought it possible for the plane to go, but Lindsay on my left was lagging. Suddenly, to my shock, his aircraft lurched away to port, obviously hit. I saw it receive another burst of deadly fire. One of his engines started smoking and in horror I saw the aircraft climb vertically, roll, and spin down to crash into the water in an explosion of flames. No one could survive such a plunge. It all took a few seconds.

Now Ralph and I raced into a welcome bank of low cloud. I headed eastwards over Turkey, making for the hills and flying pell-mell down the valleys between the mountains. In a short time I knew we were flying alone and the 109 had broken off the attack. His attention to Lindsey's plane had given us time to escape. We landed safely back at base after being airborne for four and a half hours.

There was bad news to come. It was the Doc who told me that Arthur Horsfall was reported missing together with his navigator Roger Colley. Someone on the sortie thought they had made radio contact with him after we got out over Turkey, but the reply had been uncertain. Nothing more had been heard of him since then. I was stunned to hear the news. That night I slept badly, on my own in the tent with Arthur's camp bed nearby, alert for the sound of him coming in. I had a terrible headache, and at one point was physically sick. In the morning I awoke feeling dreadful. Initially, it was presumed that Arthur must have either crashed or force-landed in Turkey. The day wore on with no news about him forthcoming, and at the end of the afternoon the CO asked me to pack up his kit and personal belongings and put them in stores; a sad task indeed, and one that has haunted me since. My heart was at rock bottom as I picked up Arthur's sun glasses and put them away in his case. I folded his khakis and best blue uniform along with the other things that were RAF issue and put them on one side. Folding his pyjamas and then putting away his shaving gear into his leather toilet case was particularly hard. These were such personal items. I felt awkward and miserable, feeling I was intruding on Arthur's space, but the thing had to be done. He had a photograph album and a five-year diary. I put these under his clothes without looking at them. If he was to come back, I wanted him to be sure I hadn't looked at any of his things. I continued to try and hope that he had got away and was safe somewhere, but my heart was very heavy. In fact, we all knew that the whole show was very bad, and it stuck in our gullet that we were still not managing to be effective and drop bombs on the targets. We simply did not have the fighter aircraft to meet the huge resources the Luftwaffe were putting into the offensive and our Beaus felt inadequate against the Me 109s. Apparently, the Island of Leros was still holding out, but our hearts were heavy for our troops on the ground. We had seen first-hand what a pounding they were getting from the air.

As always, we put the best face we could on things. Tex had arrived back from Idku in the morning with some mail, bringing a grand Christmas parcel for me from my friend Joyce. In the evening, in my empty tent, I dressed in my best blue and had a night in town with the boys. There was still no news of Arthur when I got back.

I was very disappointed the next day to find out that though Dave Crerar's cine-camera photographs of the Heinkel came out OK, mine

Flt Sgt Roger Colley stands in front of his Beaufighter 'T', 46 Squadron, at Lakatamia, Cyprus, 1943. Bryan Wild with Ralph Gibbons also flew this plane on 21 September and 12 October that year.

were blank; it seemed that unfortunately my camera had jammed. It was clear from these that Dave's fire had hit the Heinkel on the wing tip. Dave promised to give me a copy of his photos, and as he got in the first shots on the Heinkel, it fell out that Dave claimed the Heinkel, and I claimed a 'damaged'. I learned from Bill Kemp that he had circled Lindsey's plane after it crashed, but saw only petrol tanks floating on the sea. He also said he had seen all the action and agreed that Dave and I had both hit the Heinkel: his shots had kicked up some debris from the plane on the wing, and I had hit the fuselage. He was happy to give me the whole claim, but we left it at that. It didn't seem that important in relation to the losses. There was still no news of Arthur or Roger Colley.

The signal came through on 18 November 1943 that the daylight detachment at Cyprus was being closed down. Leros had finally fallen to the enemy, its thousands of British and other allied troops killed in the fighting or taken captive. It appeared that with this defeat, the attempt to retain the Dodecanese Islands was effectively over.

8

Christmas and New Year in North Africa

The Heinkel which Dave Crerar and Bryan Wild shot down on 14th November 1943 has now been identified as being from 6 Staffel of KG100, flown by Uffz Walter Pink, known to the Germans to have been lost north of Leros. It was flying from Kalamaki, Greece. Two of the crew survived the crash and were rescued by the Germans; the other two died: the pilot, Uffz Walter Pink, was wounded and rescued; Fw Kurt Bruder (Observer) was listed as missing and his body was not recovered; Fw Johann Sonnenschein (Wireless Operator) was wounded and rescued; Uffz Helmut Grundke (Air Gunner) was listed as killed, so presumably his body was recovered.

Nearly 300 British aircrew were killed in the Dodecanese campaign, and the Germans claimed they took as many as 13,000 British and Italian prisoners from Kos and Leros.

With the end of the Dodecanese Campaign, the Squadron resumed its patrol, intruder and convoy duties, continuing to harass the enemy in the Mediterranean.

It seemed to take for ever to get back to base. A Lodestar transport plane took us to Heliopolis, but not enough Beaus arrived the next day to ferry us all, so I stayed behind with the kit. No plane arrived for me, so I got the train back to Alex, and the Doc picked me up in the ambulance. 'There's a big flap on at Idku,' he said. 'Some highly secret moves by the Air Ministry are afoot. One attachment has already gone.' He knew no more detail, so I asked him a much more important question. 'How's my cat?' I knew I could not leave Timbaki at Lakatamia, so had found a friendly DC3 pilot who agreed to take him over to Idku for me. 'How's your cat indeed!' Doc said. 'He's settling in as if he owns the place. We now have four cats and three dogs in the Mess, would you believe, and I reckon he might end up being CO.'

Coming back to base brought mixed feelings. It was great to be back. But on the other hand there was the other empty half of my tent, where

Arthur should have been. Jack Barnes read my mind, and invited me over to share with him. I was very grateful to him for that.

The CO, Tommy Scade, congratulated our Lakatamia detachment in the morning. 'I've some good news for you,' he said. 'You will be collecting new Mark VIII Beaus tomorrow to start training. There will be some moves shortly for the Squadron and maybe some action, so let's make sure we're ready for anything.' The Mark VIIIs were called the long-nosed Beau because of an extra 'blister' on the front, which housed more efficient radar equipment. That evening I put on my best blues and went into Alex with Jenx and Butch Charles, meeting up later with the Doc in Maxims over steak and chips. The Doc was in fine form. 'The RAF moves in mysterious ways its wonders to perform,' he said, leaning back in his seat. 'Here we are, all wondering what's coming next. As for me, I'm just going to concentrate a wee while on digesting this steak.'

'It's wonderful steak, isn't it?' said Jenx. 'As long as we can still get to Maxim's we'll be fine. It's got all the best of a bar and a restaurant combined.'

'Ach, well,' said Doc, 'You'll find that after the war, this will catch on. Folks like us will come back home with stories of steak and chips in the bar, and before too long we'll be going up to the barmaid in the Blithering Arms at Much Wallop in the Marsh, or wherever, and we'll be ordering our dinner with our pint.'

'It'll never happen,' I said, laughing at the very thought. 'Not in Britain. We'll be back to just the drinks and the pork scratchings for ever more, Amen.'

'He's right,' said Jack. 'I can't imagine asking the landlord in my home town for a steak and kidney pie and mashed potatoes, oh, and a pint of ale to wash it down, please!' The concept seemed incredible to us. But the Doc was insistent.

'You mark my words, it will happen. Pubs with food. After the war, things will change. Remember I said it first. Now, who's for ice cream?'

Dudley Arundel flew me down to 'Kilo 40' aerodrome near Cairo on 21st November to collect a new Mk VIII Beau. I took off in the new job about 10.00 and found her shaking like a leaf, but flew her back to Idku, with Flt Sgt Lloyd as my Number 2. I don't think either of us found it a very comfortable experience. However, I took off again in the afternoon to drop Lloyd back at Kilo 40 and return to base. While the kite went into maintenance to fix the problem, Ralph and I had to study instructional films and attend short courses on how to use the new radar system. A Flight Sergeant Sykes came up to give Ralph some one-to-one gen on the set. It took Ralph a while to get used to it, and we carried out many practice aerial exercises to get the new radar technique up to speed. Once we could comfortably fly the new Beau with the radar system we knew that we would have no difficulty in picking up low flying bandits. We soon got into it, and by now Ralph was back to his old self and we were settled back together again pretty well.

There were only a few operational scrambles for the Squadron in December, and nearly all of them turned out to be friendlies. For the rest of the time we continued with exercises, NFTs, and CGIs. Ralph and I had fun on one naval exercise involving practice attacks on HMS *Penelope*, now resting in Alex harbour. Jenx was also an attacker. The fighters were spitfires but we managed to make three interceptions without being seen, which was rather satisfying.

The lack of operational flying meant that for the next few weeks I had plenty of time on my hands for leisure activities. December was launched in grand style when we went to see the dance band 'Geraldo and his Orchestra' at the station cinema, which was packed to suffocation. Dorothy Carless and Doreen Villiers were there in person; big names at the time. It was even more impressive to us because the second half of the show was 'on the air' and we felt that the world was listening. After that we seemed to have a string of surprise guests. First came an Italian Savoia-Marcheitti 82 (SM 82) in the new 'Free Italian' colours. The Mess emptied as we all rushed out to take a good look at it. The crew stayed with us a few days. A German Fieseler 'Storch' also landed, bearing our colours; an interesting aircraft, fitted with dust filters and full desert survival equipment. This plane had been flown over to the British by a couple of German privates about two weeks before; we hoped this might be indicative of German morale generally. After these the Americans arrived; first in a US Baltimore, and two days later a B-25 Mitchell bomber. All the crew members stayed with us and were entertained in the Officers Mess, adding an amount of pizzazz to the proceedings. I was introduced to a new concept: I was given a dollar bill signed by some of the crew, and learned that if I ever failed to produce it at their request, I would be required to buy them a drink. Thus I became a 'Short Snorter'. The Americans repaid our hospitality by inviting those of us who wanted to go up for a trip in the Mitchell. I went on board with Tommy Scade, Dudley Arundel, Doc MacDonald and Harry Doodson. The pilots among us got a chance to handle the plane in flight, and this went down in our log books as 'dual instruction'. On another day I enjoyed taking the Tiger Moth to Heliopolis, Cairo, to pick up Dave Crerar. I let him fly it back and took pleasure in the sense of flying along at its gentler pace, without hurry and at ease. There was football to enjoy and I continued to play a lot of bridge; when I totted up my winnings at the end of December it came to around 225 pesetas, quite a hoard. Ralph played with us a couple of times but for the most part I played with Owen, Flight Officer Armitage and 'Nelson' Keys. 'You're getting too good, Oscar,' said Armitage, handing over his losses one evening. 'You lucky blighter; you can jolly well buy the next round.'

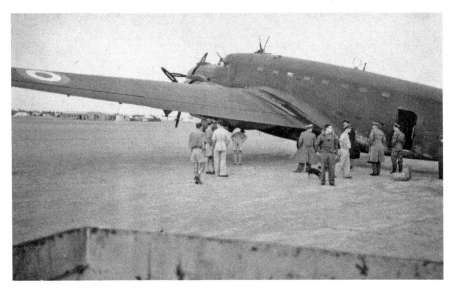

Italian Savoia-Marchetti (SM 82), photographed at Idku in Egypt where it landed early December 1943 (the Italians had signed the Armistice in September that year). The pilot exchanged his 'wings' badge with Bryan Wild, and it is still in Bryan's family today. The SM 82) was an Italian transport aircraft that was also capable of being used in a bombing role. It was able to carry approximately up to 8,000 lbs in an assorted load. The aircraft was powered by three Alfa Romeo engines and was built in two levels with the top (wooden) floor being fitted with up to thirty-two seats, while the lower level carried bombs or freight. It normally had a crew of four with two pilots, an engineer and a mechanic air gunner. It was used more often as a transport aircraft than in its bombing role as it had a cruising speed of only 160 mph and a maximum ceiling of approximately 16,000 feet, it was easy prey for allied fighters.

German Storch at Idku, in the first week of December 1943. It was understood that this aircraft had been flown over to the allies by a couple of German privates two weeks before. The Storch was a slow-flying liaison or observation plane.

US 'Marauder' Idku 1944; a speedy, medium bomber.

US Marauder tail
plane showing
guns.

We had many ways to keep our spirits up. Sometimes when everything was quiet and we were feeling a bit flat, someone in the Mess—usually Jack Barnes—would pipe up: 'Things aren't so bad after all,' and then Dudley Arundel would take up the trail: 'You say that, but they've pulled down the old pub,' to one or two boos from the people sitting around. And Jack would reply, 'But they're putting up a larger one!'

'Hooray,' someone would shout. Dudley would continue: There's only one bar.'

'Boo!'—from a growing number of voices.

'But it's a hundred yards long!' Jack would reply.

'Hooray!' from the chorus.

'You can only buy one glass of beer,' says Dudley, in disgust.

'Boo!'

'It holds a gallon!' says Jack.'

'Hooray!' By this time everyone would be joining in and laughing. Now from the back, the Scottish voice of the Doc would chip in mournfully. 'Maybe so. But you can't buy any whisky.'

'Boo!'

'That's because they're giving it away free!' Jack would cry.

'Hooray!'

From this point onwards, suggestions and replies would be coming from all sides:

'You can't get one over the eight.'

'Boo!'

'You can get one over the eighty!'

'Hooray!'

'The landlord's a shocker.'

The chorus in the background was now rather deafening and delivered with a melodramatic change in tone. 'Boo!' they intoned, deeply and derisively.

'But the landlady's a scorcher!' The responding 'Hooray' was like listening to a football crowd, and it went on for rather a long time.

'That's all very well,' Sheriff Muir says, wagging his finger, 'But you can stop your cheering because the pub closes at six.'

Jack jumps in quickly and shouts triumphantly, 'In the morning!'

This time the cheers were deafening and everyone was laughing so much that even the Sheriff and the Doc couldn't keep their faces straight any longer. This was usually followed by a rush to the bar. Spirits restored, as it were.

The outstanding feature of the month, however, was the number of parties. The Christmas spirit took us early and we were in the mood to celebrate; and that meant celebrating anything that came to hand. 'It's my father's birthday today,' I said to Jack Barnes, as we walked towards the Mess for lunch on 2nd December. 'Hey, everybody,' said Jack, entering the room, 'It's Oscar's father's birthday today. Let's celebrate!' Three days later it was my own birthday, so that evening there was another lively session in the mess. The Italian crew were still with us, and the pilot slapped me on the back, shook my hand and drank my health. He was a friendly soul, and he unpinned his wings badge and gestured it towards me. 'Swap?' he said. 'Happy birthday.'

The next week was the Officer's Mess Party on the 10th December. This was a big affair for the Squadron, with around fifty guests invited to a dance and a buffet supper. Owen's Cairo West detachment was now closed and all the aircraft returned to base, so the Squadron had its full complement. We spent all morning decorating the mess with whatever we could find; mostly palm leaves, which looked marvellous, I thought. In the afternoon I put on best blue and went into Alex in the CO's car, with Dudley Arundel, Jenx, Jack Barnes and Atkins. We had a few drinks at the Cecil to get in the swing of things and then picked up the invited Wrens from the 'wrennery' and took them to Idku with us in style in the three-tonner. The party was one to remember. There were plenty of girls and eats to keep us all happy. The RAF band had been brought in from Aboukir and we danced the evening away in the open under a brilliant moon. It was a magical setting. Timbaki the cat weaved his way in and out amidst the crowd as if he was the one throwing the party, and was very popular with all the folks, particularly the wrens. I had injured my leg earlier in the week playing football, so I'm not sure how good my dancing was, but I thoroughly enjoyed the evening and when I took the wrens back home around 11.30 I was sorry it was all over. One would think that the next day would be a quiet one, but nothing like it. Spirits were still high and there was a terrific session in the Mess at lunchtime, while Sqn Ldr Arundel in the Tiger Moth, and Wg Cdr Kain in his Spitfire, beat the mess up all afternoon. Things were just winding down when Doc said to Jack Barnes. 'You look a bit rough. Didn't you get a shave this morning?'

Jack always had a lot of dark stubble. He rubbed his chin. 'Maybe. Maybe not. But I tell you what. I bet you I can sport a decent beard in fifteen minutes.'

'I didn't go through medical school for nothing,' said the Doc. 'It means I know it can't be done; so you'll have to cheat. You've borrowed a false theatrical beard from ENSA and hidden it under your jacket, and you're not getting my hard-earned money that way.'

'No, no,' said Jack. 'No borrowed false beards, I assure you. OK, everybody. The Doc is too old and too wise to risk his pay. Who else will take me on? The deal is: if I'm not sporting a full beard in fifteen minutes,

I buy you a drink. But if I have a face full of bristles....' He looked round and grinned. 'You buy the next round.'

'OK,' I said. 'You're on. Fifteen minutes by the clock.'

There was an ash tray on the table filled with stub ends and beside it an almost full box of matches. Jack opened the box, struck a match, and blew it out once the sulphur on the end had burnt. Then, almost immediately, he clapped the end onto the stubble on his chin, where to my amazement it stuck. Quickly he lit another and did the same, and another and another until his whole chin was bristling with matchsticks. He looked utterly ridiculous and everyone was in stitches, myself included. 'Ta da!' he said, finally. 'Behold my beard, and two minutes left. The drinks are on Oscar, everyone.' I tried to protest. 'You said a decent beard, and that's anything but decent.' But I was drowned out in the noise of the rush to the bar. When I came back, eventually, to my table, the Doc's eyes twinkled as he raised his glass of Cyprus brandy.

'You knew about that, didn't you?' I said.

'Och, yes. Seen him do it loads of times. Always goes down a storm. Cheers.'

The Mess sessions continued, celebrating obscure relations' birthdays and anniversaries when we ran out of more immediate events. There was another ENSA show and a terrific session afterwards. In the middle of all this, two new flights were formed, with Squadron Leaders Arundel and Hooker in charge. I was pleased to land up in 'B' Flight with Owen; it meant more bridge at the flight when there was nothing doing during the night and we were hanging around with no action. I met a rather nice wren called Pamela Grindley and met up with her in Alex a few times, and we invited a party of wrens back to the Mess one evening for tea. There was so little operational flying that it felt rather like a real Christmas holiday. On Christmas Eve there was a massive 'binge' in the Mess and the high spirits got out of hand somewhat. Some of the boys started a tie-cutting session. As I tried to protest at Owen Hooker cutting the end off my 'second' tie, which I had lent to another person, he pushed me back and as I slid down the wall with my back to it, my hand was gashed on a piece of broken glass. Blood poured all over the place. Doc Macdonald had had a lot to drink, but he and Doc Ferris of 247 Squadron, still in merry mood, rushed me off to sick-quarters, and stood over me chatting and joking while Doc Lowe put three stitches in. I spent Christmas day with my hand bandaged up and my arm in a sling but as usual thoroughly enjoyed the traditional visiting to and fro from one mess to another and the good food provided.

Between Christmas and New Year we even had an invitation to be guests at an Arab wedding at the Bella Vista Hotel in Alex. All the boys were included so a large party of us went, and it turned out to be a most remarkable and

Lunchtime session in the Mess. Doc MacDonald's caption on the reverse reads: 'Taken after a lunchtime session. I am on the piano with Sherriff Muir behind me and Oscar Wild standing up. Charlie Peace with Fritz in the foreground'.

10 December 1943, Christmas party in the Mess, decorated with palm trees. Charlie Peace easily recognizable, seated on the floor, front.

hilarious experience. This was a warm-up for the final party of the year: the New Year's Eve dance. The night before there had been an ENSA show, and many of the members stayed on for it. Together with the wrens, this made around seventy guests in all, and the biggest Squadron party ever. As before, after helping to decorate the Mess, I drove over to Alexandria with Jack Barnes and collected some of the wrens from the Sacre Coeur in Alexandria. It was a splendid evening. There had been a lot of rain over the previous weeks, so a large marquee was erected, and there was a huge bonfire outside. Once again the RAF Dance Band from Aboukir played for us. As midnight was counted down, Doc MacDonald made a dramatic entrance through the front door of the Mess dressed as an ancient old man, representing 1943, and was booed and heckled as he made his way through the crowded room and out at the back door. He was in fact the oldest member of the Squadron and, as it happened, I was the youngest. I therefore landed the job of representing the New Year, 1944, and, as the Doc exited bang on midnight, a flaming punch was served, and in I came, dressed as a baby with sheets for a nappy, and cheered to the nines. Not my finest hour, and no one from ENSA took my details for future bookings, but great fun all the same. We just about managed to squeeze everyone into a huge circle to sing Auld Lang Syne. It was 1.30 in the morning when Jack Barnes and I took our three wrens back into Alex. As Jack snoozed on the way home, I reflected on a year full of strange and powerful experiences. As I turned the car into the camp at 3.30 a.m., I knew that despite all the difficult things I had seen and been through, I was actually having the time of my life.

On 9 January 1944, I and four other crews were airborne in the afternoon bound for a new detachment at Tocra, a desert aerodrome on the coast near Benghazi in Libya, mainly to provide night cover to the Mediterranean convoys. This meant the Squadron was now back to its proper role as a night-fighter outfit. As before, the convoys were escorted by a small fleet of warships. The others in the group were the leader, Sqn Ldr Owen Hooker, Flt Lt Bradwell, WO Boswell and Flt Sgt Lacey, and of course their navigators. I very quickly decided there was too much wind at this place. Furthermore, the facilities at Tocra were basic tents and it was quite something to manage to get a wash. The showers were often cold, and sometimes days passed before I felt properly clean.

For the next few months Ralph and I carried out plenty of missions from Tocra and also from another desert aerodrome at El Adem, near Tobruk, Libya, where we had a sub-detachment. Often I would go to bed in my Mae West in the knowledge that a large convoy had been sighted, but there were few scrambles and the patrols were fairly straightforward. When we were at El Adem we messed with 41 Squadron, and as the days went by I struck up several friendships with these day-fighter pilots. On one occasion they let me test one of their Hurricanes, airborne for one hour: a MK.IV, with two anti-tank guns fixed to the underside of the wings.

I found the flights over the Sahara fascinating. The whole region, of course, was pure sand for hundreds of miles, and there was always a worrying thought at the back of my mind about what might happen if I was forced to make a crash landing in an area where there wasn't even an oasis. I had a small survival pack containing things like matches, a bar of chocolate, water purification tablets and a rubber bottle (in case I was lucky enough to find some water). I also carried a leaflet asking some friendly Arab to look after me. I was very glad I never had to use either of them. On another occasion, Jack Barnes and the Doc had to force-land in the desert in the Tiger Moth, but luckily not far in. It was fascinating low flying over the terrain because it was littered with the aftermath of the recent battles between Rommel and the 8th Army. All over the place there were wrecks of tanks, gun batteries, army vehicles of all kinds. Once, whilst a few friends and I were exploring on foot in an area near Benghazi, we came across a crashed Me 109 and had the chance to examine it closely.

In the middle of January I arrived back from my NFT in 'L' to find three Hurricanes of 94 Squadron parked on my hard standing. I had to clear the runway and had no alternative but to put the kite onto the soft ground, which was so uneven that I 'hogged' the plane on the rough. We had to tow her out of the mud; a terrible job. I cringed as some rivets sheared off

Aircrew examining crashed Me 109, semi-desert near Tocra, Benghazi.

Doc MacDonald (passenger) force-landed in desert area with Jack Barnes, North Africa 1944.

Jack Barnes (left) and Doc MacDonald, early 1944, were both great characters in 46 Squadron.

under the main plane. The mechanics of 136 MU came to look at it and sucked their teeth, saying they thought one of the wing spars had gone. They were very pessimistic about the whole thing and started to take the plane apart. It took a number of days, and Ralph and I stayed with 41 Squadron while it was all being done. Owen Hooker came and went from Tocra a number of times and played bridge with us and on one occasion he brought ten letters for me in the post. This helped ease the boredom, but the main compensation for being stuck at El Adem was that on the third day I managed to have a bath in one of 41 Squadron's bath tubs. It almost made it worth the wait. Ralph and I finally made it back to Tocra six days later. The plane still had problems which surfaced one after another over the following days. The first NFT identified that one weapon was bent. The next day en route to Savoia with a controller from sector on board, I had to put the plane into dive four times to get the undercarriage down. I think the controller found the trip a little too eventful! Again, two days later we had a flat tyre after landing, and an elongated arm on the port undercarriage made the plane unserviceable. Eventually Ralph and I flew 'L' to Berca, Benghazi, to get it repaired and brought it back in OK order in the evening. Finally we were ready to go, but the weather was atrocious, with high winds and torrential rain. The next day in the middle of another rain storm, a Halifax swung off the runway and pranged the stationery 'L'. When I heard the news, I put my head in my hands. The starboard wing airscrews were both written off, and my sense of injustice at our bad luck soared sky high. There was not much happening, however, apart from what turned out to be a scramble for a 'friendly', so at least we were not missing important action. We moved to a new and improved Nissen-hut site, but the days dragged, and especially so because early in the month Owen was posted back to base, his tour of service having come to a close. We all missed him. The aerodrome itself was often unserviceable because of bad weather, which continued into and through February, with either heavy rain or sandstorms, but always strong wind, sometimes as high as 40 miles an hour. In the middle of February an ingrowing toenail put me into hospital and out of action for a week. Things did not get better once I was ready to fly. On 22nd, with a Greek pilot and forty eggs on board as cargo, my brakes failed while taxiing and I collided with a bowser, leaving the plane unserviceable with a broken nose and me suffering from a lot of jokes about scrambled eggs. The nose replacement had to be flown in and the kite was out of action for nearly a week. While we were waiting, Wing Commander Tommy Scade arrived with 'Sheriff', bringing the mail. There was enough of mine stacked up to keep me busy reading it for a week.

Elsewhere the Squadron had more satisfying action than in Tocra: operating from St Jean's in Palestine, Sqn Ldr Blackburn destroyed two

Long-nosed Beaufighter MM885/J, 46 Squadron, Idku, Egypt 1943/44. Built by Bristols at Filton. Ferried to Middle East and 46 Squadron. Later, went to 108 Sqn, but suffered engine failure on take-off at Hassani (Greece), 2 February 1945, and undercarriage collapsed. *Beaufighter history detail supplied by Russell Brown*

46 Squadron Beaufighters in formation over North Africa, 1944: tail-plane of Beau MM885/J visible on left of picture.

46 Squadron Beaufighter Mk VIII 'S' shot over Delta, near Idku, Egypt.

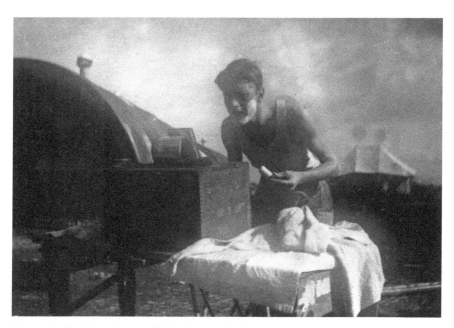

Not quite the Ritz. Bryan Wild, bathroom facilities, ?Tocra 1944.

Ju 52s and damaged a third over Calato, Rhodes; and Dave Crerar shot down a Ju 52 over Maritza on the very last day of his posting. Both of these happened on night intruder patrols in brilliant moonlight. In our outpost in Tocra we raised a celebratory toast to their success.

I was thankful to be posted back to Idku at the end of February and saw out the last day of the month cheerfully in Alexandria, travelling in with the Doc and Jack Barnes in Stan Broadbent's car. Owen had gone to England, and now I flew Dave Crerar and his RO Butch Charles to Heliopolis to set them on their way home as well. Many of the same gang were still propping up the bar, however. I got a rapturous welcome from Timbaki, who was still sharing hosting duties with Charlie Peace's Daschund, Fritz. There was an ENSA play 'Ladies in Waiting' at Idku early in the month and when the cast were entertained in the Mess afterwards, these two characters did their bit in endearing 46 Squadron to the visitors. With Timbaki's help I was introduced to the actresses Anne Castle and Kay Livingstone and we arranged to meet in Alexandria some days later.

Our task now was to carry out night intruder raids on German-occupied Rhodes. On 4 March 1944, Ralph and I were briefed at 16.00 hours to target Calato, the main aerodrome on Rhodes. The reconnaissance photographs we received for these missions showed our targets in great detail, including the damage of previous war activity around the

Bryan Wild, January 1944, Idku.

Halifaxes at El Adem, Tobruk, early 1944.

aerodromes. We were airborne at 21.00 hours on a very clear moonlight night, feeling very happy to have left the Tocra weather behind us. I flew at 400 feet all the way, arriving at Calato at 22.45. We patrolled the bay and spotted nothing of note, shipping or aircraft, but powerful searchlights from Rhodes Town picked up the Beau twice and some thankfully inaccurate ack-ack appeared nearby. Near the end of the patrol, Ralph thought he saw an aircraft behind us, so I evaded violently just in case it was one of their night-fighters. We returned and pancaked at 1.30 a.m. The total time of the mission was 4.30 hours. Three days later I made a second visit to Calato with a similar result: nothing of note.

There was more enemy engagement elsewhere. On 5th March, Sheriff Muir was flying with Group Captain Max Aitken when they shot down three Ju 52s and damaged another, which raised all our spirits and our own hopes of increasing the count.

On 7 March 1944, Flight Officer Angus Taylor DFC and Charlie Peace were airborne at 01.35 in the morning for intruder operations over Cos, but they failed to return. There was a huge search for them, Wing Commander Scade and four other aircraft searching the area at first light with no success. Tommy Scade went out again after a brief touchdown at base, this time with myself and Squadron Leader Blackburn. We saw some oil and a yellow object, possibly a raft or dinghy on the water, and we directed a motor launch to it; but whatever it turned out to be, it was empty, and we had to conclude that Angus and Charlie were gone. Another deeply felt loss for me in Charlie, a real character who I had known since my Blackpool days. It was made even more poignant by the fact that I now took over the care of Fritz. He stayed with me until I left the Squadron, which was not long. The very next day I heard I was due to be posted home soon; my tour was nearly finished.

I had only one more operational flight—an intruder over Maritza on 12th March, in rain and lightning—and by 16th March, intruder operations were finished for that period of the moon. I met up with Anne Castle and Kath Livingston quite regularly, playing a lot of tennis with them and either Stan Broadbent or Clark Hickman at the Sporting Club. I made a short visit to Tocra with Wing Commander Tommy Scade, as his observer, of all things, since of course he knew the way pretty well on his own and didn't need my help, and for the rest of the time I had a routine of NFTs and mainly quiet nights on duty, punctuated by the usual Liberty run into Alex with the crowd. I was finally posted with Ralph, Jenx, Plt Off. Silvester, WO Kendall, and WO Lloyd on 28th March. It meant saying some painful goodbyes to close friends, particularly Doc Macdonald and Jack Barnes among all the rest of the 46 Squadron boys. We caught the train from Alex to Cairo in the afternoon, landing up at 22 Personnel Transit Camp. There we heard we were all going home to the UK, and by air. We spent the rest of the day celebrating.

Bryan Wild (left) in Alexandria with ENSA members Ann Castle and Kath Livingston, March 1944, and possibly either Stan Broadbent or Clark Hickman on the right. Ann Castle continued her career in films, and later appeared in *The Shooting Party* (1985) and Stephen Spielberg's *Empire of the Sun* (1987).

Reconnaissance photograph, Maritza, Rhodes, 12 March 1944, showing parked German aircraft and evidence of previous bombing including extensive damage to the hangars.

Spitfire and Beaufighter 46 Squadron at El Adem, near Tobruk, North Africa, January or February 1944.

Bryan Wild's close friend, Squadron Leader Owen Hooker, with 46 Squadron mascot Fritz, Idku, early in 1944. Fritz was left behind by the Germans and adopted by 'Charlie' Peace. Ironically, the German Daschund became 46 Squadron's mascot.

We should have known that the process of posting was not so straightforward. By April 6th after umpteen false starts and stops en route, we had already been stuck in Casablanca for three days. That night, when we reported to the transit desk at 17.00 we found we were listed for the plane home. There we sat, waiting, until one by one all six of us were crossed off to make way for brass hats. 'Brass hats; brassed off!' said Jenx, in disgust. The next night, though, we made it. A Skymaster DC4 took off with us at 2100 hours and we pancaked at Prestwick on Saturday 8th April at seven in the morning; more than nine hours later. It was pouring with rain but it was a glorious feeling to be back in the UK. The green, green grass and leafy trees—the feeling was marvellous. I arrived home in Bolton just in time for dinner on Easter Sunday.

9

Mosquitos over Europe

In 27 January 1944 the 872-day Siege of Leningrad was broken. Nearly 1.5 million Soviets had died, but overall the Soviet army was overpowering the Germans and driving them out of their territories. At the same time, the RAF was systematically bombing German cities, and 27 January saw the most concentrated night raid of the war on Berlin, with 75 bombs falling on the city every minute. The war in the Far East was also raging. At home for the next five months, the build up to D-Day was in progress, and on 6 June, the Allies invaded Normandy. The Allied air offensive totalled 13,743 planes, of which nearly 5,500 were fighters. During the Normandy campaign, 2,000 RAF aircraft were lost, with over 8,000 air crew. By October 1944 when Bryan Wild was posted to 25 Squadron, the Germans were on the defensive in France, the Allies were in the Low Countries, and on the last day of September, all the German cross-channel guns had been captured. Rumania and Finland had both signed an armistice in September. Now the RAF onslaught on Germany was relentlessly continued. The Mosquito was one of the fastest fighter planes in the world at that time, an effective night-fighter cover for the bombers over Europe.

After a fine spell of two weeks' leave, I was posted to No.51 OTU Cranfield, near Bedford, Bucks, as a flying instructor. The aircraft were Beauforts and Beaufighters. I was now separated from Ralph Gibbons, who was going to be trained as an instructor himself, so it felt as if the last connection with 46 Squadron had gone, but I was overjoyed to find my old friend from 46 Squadron there as a Flight Commander, Sqn Ldr Owen Hooker. Edward "Sludge" Ledwidge was also here, briefly. There was also another very close friend from the past, from Squires Gate, WO Deryk Hollinrake. Cranfield was a peace-time RAF station with traditional red brick buildings and first-rate Officers Mess and sleeping quarters: a real change after the tents at Idku. There was a local pub nearby called the 'Swan', and I spent many happy hours here, where the thing was playing

DC3 North Africa 1944, the workhorse transport aircraft.

the local farmers at darts. I also managed to play quite a lot of cricket for the Station cricket team. Nearby was Woburn Abbey, which was then a 'Wrennery'. Things were looking up.

For about three weeks, I could only instruct on Beaufighters whilst waiting to attend a Flying Instructors Course. Deryk Hollinrake was busy teaching the new ROs the skills of radar. The 'pupils' learning to become night-fighters were former experienced day-fighter pilots of the single-engined Spitfires and Hurricanes. Now that day bombing raids had more or less ceased, day fighters were not needed in such quantities; hence the change. Although these pilots were very experienced on single-engined fighters, and had also been trained on the twin-engined Oxford, they found the big, heavy Beaufighter a very different proposition. But before flying this machine, they had to receive dual instruction on the Beauforts.

On May 17th 1944, I attended a three-week course for flying instructors at No. 3. Flying Instructors' School at Lulsgate Bottom near Bristol, where I flew Oxfords and went through the 'patter' which eventually I would have to impart to my pupils. After a short leave at home, I returned to Cranfield as a qualified flying instructor, now with the rank of Flight Lieutenant. First, I had to learn to fly the Beaufort, the fore-runner of the Beaufighter, so that I could give dual instruction (both pilots sat side by side). The pupil would be given several lessons on the Beaufort, culminating with a 'Beau demo' before going solo. I gave the 'Beaufighter Demo' to two pupils at a time. They stood in the well behind me while I put the aircraft through its paces. On the whole they were usually very impressed by its performance. I remembered the time Wg Cdr Adams did the same for me back in Blackpool; a long time ago, it seemed.

From April to October, 1944, I clocked up many flying hours in Beauforts and Beaufighters instructing. Altogether, I recorded over 140 hours on the Beaufort; 24 hours on the Beau. I thoroughly enjoyed my stay at this 'drome, finding the crews friendly and the local people extremely anxious to be hosts. The CO was Sqn Ldr W. R. L. Beaumont, a popular and well-known character in RAF circles, and with Owen Hooker as one of my flight commanders I considered myself very fortunate in my posting. In the middle of this six-month spell the momentous D-Day landings took place in Normandy, but being in the training unit meant I was not involved in the action. On the 10th October, after a short leave, Deryk Hollinrake and I were posted together to 25 Squadron, Coltishall, near Norwich, Norfolk. The aircraft was the De Havilland Mosquito. I was extremely pleased to be paired up with Deryk, but on the other hand, before leaving Cranfield we had to say goodbye to Owen Hooker. Sadly, I did not meet him again: the New Zealander returned to his native land after the war.

October 1944, No. 25 Squadron, Coltishall, Norfolk

In early October, Deryk Hollinrake and I arrived at Coltishall by car, an Austin Ten which I had purchased at Bedford. Like Cranfield, this was a well-known aerodrome built before the war with brick buildings in the standard RAF peacetime mode. The CO was Wg Cdr Mitchell. I was placed in 'A' Flight, the Flight Commander being Sqn Ldr William Hoy DFC.

I had never flown a Mosquito before. Deryk and I were fascinated by our first inspection of it. It was a mainly-wooden construction, much lighter than other aircraft; a twin-engined plane that was both fast and versatile, with capability as a day- or night-fighter, bomber or reconnaissance. The Mosquito's maximum speed was 300 to 400 mph, making it the fastest aircraft in the world at that time. It had a range of nearly 2,000 miles and could climb to over 30,000 feet on its Rolls Royce Merlin engines. The night-fighter version which we were to fly was armed with four cannons and four machine guns and had extra radar equipment; the very latest system for interception, a 'tail looking' scanner, and a built-in radar-operated homing device. The weight of this additional equipment reduced the speed somewhat in comparison to the day-fighter, but it was still ahead of the rest of the field. The cockpit array of instruments and controls was impressive. Deryk and I were amazed to find that the bullet-proof windscreen had a high-speed wiper. In this aircraft the pilot and radio operator sat side by side, the entrance to the cockpit being a door on the starboard side of the front fuselage. The RO sat on the right near the door—lucky devil—first out in case of abandoning the aircraft. 'I see they've put you near the door,' I said to Deryk.

'That's because I'm more important than you,' he said.

'No, it's because you're slower and need a head start.' We both laughed. We were full of admiration for our new kite. Its overall design was stunning, like a smooth shark camouflaged in green and grey.

My first flight in the Mossie was with Sqn Ldr Hoy on 11th October 1944, when he gave me a 25-minute demo of its capabilities, and immediately after that I went solo in another 25-minute trip. As I stepped out of the aircraft, Deryk and I were talking excitedly about its performance. It was fine to handle and the acceleration was absolutely breath-taking.

I had only just settled in at Coltishall when I had an embarrassing incident whilst taxying, only ten days after my arrival. The wing tip of my Mosquito caught the sandbagged wall of a bomb bay in which aircraft

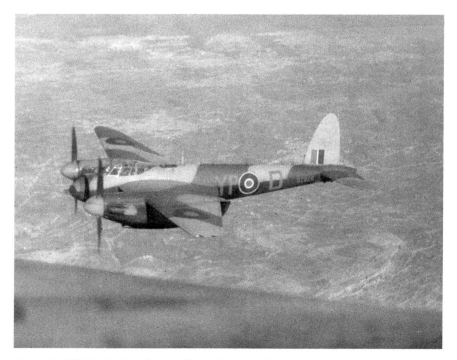

Mosquito YP-D, 23 Squadron; official photograph. After leaving 46 Squadron, Sgt. Ralph Gibbons flew in this particular aircraft as RO with Flt Lt McAlpine on at least three occasions while with 23 Squadron in 1944 and 1945. His log book entry for an operational flight in YP-D on 14 April 1945 reads, 'Neuruppin. Prang by 6 a/c 23 Sqdn. 5th in with 80 x 4 lb incendiaries. Fires started. All hit aerodrome. Saw Potsdam prang,' (sic). It is possibly wholly coincidental that Bryan Wild included this official photograph of a Mosquito in his collection. *Crown Copyright, Ministry of Defence.*

were parked. The damage was slight, but my pride was dented. It resulted in me being hauled before the CO of the North Weald Sector, Gp Cpt. G. L. Denholm, for a reprimand, and an endorsement in my log book in red ink, which was signed by the CO and said, 'Gross Carelessness, whilst taxying'. This took place in Wg Cdr Mitchell's office, dated October 22nd. I remembered Sgt Allan on my very first flight in the Tiger Moth back in 1940 telling me to take great care to move slowly and carefully and watch out for obstacles on taxying, and I was glad he wasn't present to add his comment.

The war with Germany had now reached a critical stage, a case of swings and roundabouts when trying to assess who had the upper hand. Certainly, the British and American armies in France were beginning to push the enemy back bit by bit from the Normandy beaches, and Russia had the German armies on the run. But here and there were worrying setbacks: Arnhem, for instance, and then in December, German troops led by Field Marshal von Rundstedt broke through the lines at the Ardennes Forest and lunged again towards Belgium. In September, Hitler had launched his new terror weapon on London: the silent, long range, rocket with a one-ton warhead. However, on the other side of the world, the Americans were beginning to win the Pacific war against the Japanese, and during October, General Douglas MacArthur had returned to the Philippines with a formidable army. For the next few months there seemed to be a lull in enemy activity. Perhaps we were beginning to win the day—and night.

The squadron was part of the strategy to combat the menace of Hitler's V1 flying bombs. It was given the task of trying to shoot down the Heinkels which were flying in low from Holland with their flying bomb slung under the starboard wing. Originally the enemy had started launching these small, pilotless, jet-propelled rockets from sloping ramps sited in various countries across the Channel. Now they were launching them from aircraft in mid-flight, and they were doing huge damage over London. Several other Mosquito night-fighter squadrons were drafted in to combat the menace of the flying bombs, because this aircraft was fast enough to catch them. They had many successes, and Hawker Tempest outfits were even more effective. But we were detailed to deal solely with the Heinkels which were carrying the bombs. The idea was to be sent on patrol way out over the North Sea, and wait there to try to intercept the Heinkels. The German pilots had adopted an efficient method of bringing the bombs to target. From their bases they flew at full speed very low over the North Sea to avoid our radar until they were about fifty miles from the English coast, when they suddenly climbed to around 3,000 feet and released the missiles on course towards London. As soon as the bombs were released, the mother aircraft would turn round, dive to sea level and return at full throttle back to Europe. It was left to other fighter aircraft such as Tempests or Typhoon single-engined fighters to chase the flying bomb while we were to deal with the Heinkels. In my case, I found the patrols most infuriating because of our strict orders that my group should ignore the V1s. During the next two months, I carried out ten such patrols in which we were nowhere near getting to grips with the launch plane: Deryk saw no enemy blip appear on his radar screen in spite of the fact that Ground Control had alerted us to the presence of a bandit on track for London. Instead, we often watched helplessly as flying bombs with the tell-tale bright orange flame trailing behind them flashed close by in the dark. We could only hope that some other Mossie or Tempest outfit would intercept and destroy them before reaching land. They were much more easily seen at night than the Heinkels, because of their burning tail of rocket fuel, but it required great skill and accuracy to shoot them down before they crossed the coast. My old friend Joe Berry on Hawker Tempests had become the top scorer at this game, shooting down around sixty altogether, and even more amazingly, on one occasion he downed seven in one single night, a staggering figure. It was extremely dangerous. The aircraft had to get in close to attack the flying rocket, and when they were successfully hit, the ensuing explosion threw debris in all directions, often hitting the attacking planes. Joe had been made Squadron Leader and Commanding Officer of 501 Squadron. At the end of October 1944, I was devastated to hear the tragic news that Joe had been killed, shot down by ground fire while flying low over Holland. Yet another loss.

However, despite our own operational limitations and the difficulties of catching sight of the mother aircraft, I did have one or two chases after Heinkels, and on one patrol we very nearly caught up with a bandit. On this particular night, March 17th 1945, we were flying in Mosquito 'G' just off the Suffolk coast. The weather was poor; cloud and rain. Ground Control suddenly called in to say the enemy was closing in low down towards Kent. We were vectored eastwards to meet it, but the bandit must have launched or jettisoned the bomb before we got there, because when Deryk suddenly picked it up as a blip on his radar he was surprised to find it was now travelling eastwards at speed back towards Germany at only 200 feet above sea level.

A chase at this altitude, in bad weather and doing well over 300 mph, was both frantic and dangerous. One false move on the stick, dipping the plane's altitude a fraction, could result in the aircraft smashing into the waves in a matter of seconds. To enable safer low level flying at speed, the boffins had invented a gadget called a radio altimeter, which helped the pilot judge his height above sea level instantly. The old Aneroid altimeter was useless under these operational conditions because it worked on a barometer principle and the time delay in registering the height was too slow. We had to know our height above sea level *instantly*, especially in a fast plane like the Mosquito. The new radio altimeter sent out split second signals down to the water which returned immediately to record the altitude. It was a marvellous bit of kit. If I knew beforehand that I was going to be flying at a very low level, I could set the altimeter to register visibly the safe height at which I wanted to fly. So if I thought that flying at 200 feet above sea level was the appropriate and safest height, I simply turned a knob on the instrument to point to 200. A yellow light would show. If I flew higher, a green would show. If I few below 200, a red light would flash and I knew I was risking my neck.

Now it came into its own. As we altered course and began the chase, I focused my awareness on the lights of the radio altimeter that I could see out of the corner of my eye, all the while concentrating on piloting the aircraft through the pitch black night in cloud, and at the same time listening intently to Deryk, who had his head buried in the radar screen following the blip and was calmly but urgently instructing me: 'He's dead ahead; we've got him. Wait ... he's drawing away. Faster, Bryan, for God's sake! That's better ... hold it ... he's jinking ... the bastard knows we're after him ... up a bit ... watch it ... watch it! We're closing fast ... Hell ... he's off the screen. Where the hell is he? He's only a few hundred feet away, damn it! Can you see anything?'

There was no way of shooting down the bandit by firing into the dark on the whim of a radar blip. I had to see the enemy aircraft with my own eyes before manoeuvring in to a viable firing position. Until that point, I was literally flying blind, straining for the faintest sight of a glowing exhaust ahead which would betray the enemy aircraft and enable me to close in.

On this particular March night with the terrible weather, we didn't see a thing. Though we had the bandit on the radar, we kept losing him. We had chased the damn thing almost to the Dutch coast before we had to give up. By the time we were on the way back our clothes were soaked in sweat from the excitement and frustration of the chase. On the way back we also saw flying bombs going past us in the dark on their way towards London, trailing their red fire.

Back in October 27th 1944 there had been a surprise move for the whole Squadron, when we were transferred to an aerodrome near Saffron Walden called Castle Camps, Cambridgeshire. This was situated out in the countryside on relatively flat land. The main buildings were much the same huts as usual, but the Officers Mess was a mansion called Walton House, just outside the aerodrome.

At this time I made friend with another pilot, Ron Pickles. He and I struck up a friendship with a local farmer at Castle Camps called Fred Tilbrook. His was a large and prosperous farm very near the aerodrome. He regularly invited aircrew to his home for good food and strong drinks, followed by endless sessions of poker or pontoon. He had several dogs, mainly Labradors and golden retrievers, and when one of them had puppies he asked us if we would like one. I loved animals. I had felt bad about leaving Fritz behind in Idku with someone else, and often wondered what happened to him. Now I was given the chance of a dog of my own, and I couldn't resist. I accepted the kind offer like a shot and called my new dog Bruce.

While I was at Castle Camps I also bought a Singer Le Mans Sport Car to replace my Austin Ten. I got it off another pilot for £44, a particularly low price because it hadn't been looked after properly. It had even been 'hand-painted' in black all over. I was no use as a mechanic, so to get it back into shape I came to an arrangement with the flight sergeant engineer: he drove it for two days a week in exchange for him renovating and maintaining it. He tuned it to perfection and always had it filled up with aircraft petrol when he handed it back. I loved that car. When I was demobbed in 1946 there was no way I could afford to run it in Civvy Street, so I took it home to Bolton, got a local man to re-spray it green for £10 and then sold it for £200.

The last quarter of 1944 had been operationally quiet, but when the German line had been pushed back after the 'Battle of the Bulge', the Allies pressed their advantage by mounting an offensive all along the Western front, and in February 1945, things changed dramatically. The aircrews were thrown into relentless night missions across the North Sea and over Germany, which continued until Germany surrendered on May 8th, Victory in Europe Day. These intensive sorties came in three distinctive types: intruder flights over Germany and occupied territories; attacking the Heinkel V1-launchers; and bomber support, escorting Lancasters on their raids into the heart of Germany to protect them from attacks by the Luftwaffe's night-fighters. Most of these flights averaged out at anything from three to four hours duration. I was engaged in seven operational flights over Germany and saw the bombing of such towns as Hamburg, Munster, Bonn, Frankfurt, Mannheim and Leipzig. Seeing the destruction going on below us through relentless bursts of ack-ack heading in our direction was an awe-inspiring and terrible sight, never to be forgotten. On several of the bomber trips we were picked up and coned by searchlights, something I found a particularly frightening experience, and fired at by anti-aircraft guns, but our plane was never hit. Occasionally, we had to be diverted on the return to England because of bad weather. Once we were sent to Brussels. On another occasion we landed at Bradwell Bay where they had the Fog Intensive Dispersal Operation (FIDO) system, and the runway edges were alight with petrol jets to beat the fog.

I also did a couple of intruder flights. On one of them, 30 March 1945, Wg Cdr William Hoy and I were detailed to make the long journey to Lista, on the Norwegian Coast; just our two aircraft. Here on a fine night we hoped to pick out some German aircraft or shipping in this enemy-occupied territory. We ended up over the airfield, looking for German planes parked around, but we were greeted by heavy and accurate flak. Unfortunately there was no joy anywhere, and we turned for home. We were not far into the journey back when suddenly William broke the mandatory radio silence. 'One of my engines has conked out,' he said to me and Deryk. 'Bad show, William!' I said, with feeling, and my heart sank down to my boots. We were about five hundred miles from home. William said, 'Will you let folks back at base know what happens if I don't make it?' That was a long flight back! Fortunately, with some remarkable flying and steady nerve on William's part, he made it back to base. The trip registered a total of five hours and twenty minutes altogether, and Hoy had flown home on one engine for roughly three hours. How good it must have felt for him to be standing on the solid ground of Saffron Walden airfield!

On April 7th, we were on an intruder sortie to Bradis, Leipzig, a round trip of 4.20 hours, when due to bad weather, we were diverted to land at Brussels. Deryk and I had a most enjoyable night walking round the city before flying back the next day. On returning to base, we learned that our stint of bomber support was coming to an end. Throughout these missions I always felt a great deal of admiration for the bomber crews. In my opinion, and indeed the opinion of most aircrews, these pilots, navigators, and gunners had the toughest of all jobs.

On one sortie I was flying low over Germany and a passenger train came in view. I sped towards it but was filled with indecision. It could be filled with German troops, but on the other hand it could be filled with civilians, maybe women and children. There were no markings, and I could not know who was inside. In the few remaining seconds I did know that I couldn't bring myself to strafe it, and we flew on.

After these operations over Germany, Deryk and I managed to obtain some leave. Deryk married June, whom he had known since his school days, and I was best man at his wedding in Todmorden. When we returned to Castle Camps, we found a distinct lull in operational activity, a sure sign that the war was leaning in our favour. By April 1945, the news was all good: Allied forces were closing in on Berlin; the Rhine had been crossed. Countries all over the world had declared war on Germany. The Japs were losing the Pacific war, on land and sea.

Bryan Wild (second from left) acted as best man at Deryk Hollinrake's wedding to June, April 1945.

The pressure eased off and we all found time for leisure pursuits: trips into Cambridge and London, for instance. A number of us saw Bolton Wanderers play Chelsea at the Chelsea ground. In London, the Air Force Club was popular, and visits to some of the well-known hotels and restaurants. One day, I walked into the Air Force Club bar and was amazed and thrilled to see Doc Macdonald, my old friend from 46 Squadron. He was now stationed at Brize Norton. It was wonderful to see him again and we agreed to keep in touch.

Then, on 30 April 1945, came the dramatic news that Hitler was dead; he had shot himself. A week later, on May 8th, Germany surrendered. That night, the whole squadron drifted into Saffron Walden to celebrate.

However, the following morning when we were still sobering up, someone reminded us all that we were still at war with Japan, and a rumour was afoot that certain crews might be posted to the Far East. Over these months, flying training was still maintained with cross-country night trips, GCI exercises, intruder practice, formation flying, etc. Sqn Ldr Dougie Greaves DFC became the Flight Commander of 'A' flight, one of the Squadron's most popular characters. William Hoy was still the CO, also very well-liked.

In July and part of August 1945, Deryk and I were sent on detachment to Bradwell Bay, Essex, on a Firing Course: Air to Air, and Air to Ground, the former exercise with drogue-towing aircraft, the latter firing at large wooden targets out to sea. We returned on 12th August, and three days later, on 15th August, the Japanese surrendered: Victory over Japan Day.

Early in September, I was called to the CO's office and, to my surprise and pleasure, Wg Cdr Hoy asked me if I would like to represent the Squadron in the first Battle of Britain Flypast over London on the 15th. 300 aircraft would be involved in the formation overall, eleven of which would be from 25 Squadron, and the whole show would be planned and led by Grp Capt Douglas Bader DSO DFC. A few days previously Bader and his wife had come to our Officers Mess dance and now there was some speculation about this. It was known that he and the Commander of Castle Camps, Wg Cdr Tim Vigors DFC, a former Battle of Britain Ace, were close friends. Had they been planning the celebration flypast then? Deryk and I were immensely proud to be involved, and for three days, 12th, 13th and 14th September, we rehearsed the formation manoeuvres, along with the other 299 aircraft led by Bader. This was all carried out over Suffolk in reasonably fine weather, but on the great day itself, September 15th, the weather was poor, with quite a lot of patchy cloud and showers, tricky for such a large formation. However, there were no real problems and the flypast was duly completed successfully. We all hoped that the royal family and the people of London, along with the hundreds of visitors along the Mall and surrounding Buckingham Palace, were impressed with the display. We certainly were. Gp Capt Bader's aircraft, quite appropriately, was a Spitfire. In later days, I saw the BBC news film of the formation, and wondered which tiny spot in the sky was my Mosquito.

Two days later, I flew for over three hours over northern Europe, on a kind of Cook's Tour to see the results of the RAF's work, also a memorable flight. There was an end-of-term feeling about things. At the end of October, Deryk Hollinrake received his demob papers and left the squadron bound for Civvy Street. From then on I had many different RO's flying with me until my turn came to be demobbed: PO MacGowan, PO Docherty; WO Jeffries; FO Baker, Flt Lt Dalton, to name a few.

I managed to obtain Christmas leave from the 19th December 1945. Whilst at home in Bolton I had time to think about the future and particularly what vocation I was going to take up. Before the outbreak of war, I had hardly been out of school, only having two years' training as a draughtsman, a job I didn't enjoy. One day, I met a valued friend and primary school head teacher, who suggested I might try teaching.

Back at Castle Camps a week later, I talked over the matter with the RAF Education Officer, who advised me to take a teachers' course when the time was ripe.

On January 10th 1946, the Squadron was transferred to Boxted, near Colchester. I wondered how I was to arrange transport for Bruce, but the CO said to me, 'Why not take him with you in the Mossie? He can go as your RO.' So Bruce flew with me in a Mosquito. He took it all in his stride, sitting beside me in the RO's seat throughout the flight, just as happy as if we were bowling along the road in my Singer sports car. He appeared in my log book in the column headed, '2nd Pilot, Pupil or Passenger'.

A new CO was now in charge of the Squadron, Sqn Ldr Goucher DFC, and Flt Lt Slater was now leading 'F' Flight. On January 2th 1946, Flt Lt Dalton (RO) and I were bound for Lubeck, Germany, for a week's duty as part of the Army of Occupation. The trip took us two hours in Mosquito 'C'. We never ventured into Lubeck whilst we were there, as the town was in a state of complete ruin. Several other crews came with us, including Dicky Goucher, and on one occasion the whole group drove into Hamburg to a famous hotel for an evening meal.

On returning to Boxted on February 2nd, I was made Flight Commander in charge of 'A' Flight. By March 21st, I had completed my very last flight in Mosquito 'T' with Flt Lt Dalton. It lasted just 35 minutes, but felt to me a momentous occasion. It seemed hard to grasp that day that my time with the RAF was over. The war was finished and a new and unmapped life lay ahead, not just for me but for all of us. As I drove away from the aerodrome on March 25th bound for Uxbridge to receive my £75 gratuity and a new suit, I was looking forward to the future, but my mind was full of vivid memories and of the many friends, both living and dead, that I was leaving behind. Or was I leaving them behind? I had a feeling they would remain with me for the rest of my life.

Notes

1. Imaginary call signs.
2. Beaufighter Marks VII and VIII: it seems these Australian variants Mark VII and VIII were never built. Bryan Wild's memoir follows his actual log book entries, countersigned by his COs, and Mark numbers are therefore left as written. It is not clear which marks of Beaufighter (and radar) were actually being operated.

Epilogue

Flight Lieutenant Bryan James Wild

Bryan James Wild was born in Yorkshire on 5th December 1921, with two brothers over a decade older than himself. His family settled in Bolton, Lancashire. Bryan was eleven when his mother died, and after completing schooling in Birmingham, where he lived with his father and step-mother, Elsie, he moved back to Bolton to make his home with his beloved Aunt Olive and Uncle Roy. The war came at an opportune time for him, faced as he was with no definite prospects and apprenticed to an occupation for which he was not well suited.

In strongly recommending him for a commission, Wing Commander Adams described Wild as: 'A very capable NCO pilot,' who showed 'great keenness to get into the air'. The Station Commander, Air Commodore W. F. Dickson stated:

> I have interviewed this NCO—he appears to be conscientious, intelligent and possessing a proper sense of responsibility. He has natural ability and is reported to have a high standard of operational efficiency. His manner is good. Generally he is of the best secondary school type with plenty of North Country shrewdness and common sense.

Shrewdness and common sense, yes, and in later life, Bryan Wild decried low flying as dangerous, invariably attributing Ack Greenwood's death to the fact that Olney was flying too low, but in 1997 AC H. C. Skinner, a colleague from Squires Gate, wrote the following in a letter to researcher Russell Brown:

> Bryan Wild was a good pilot. I remember flying along the front at Blackpool, hedge-hopping the piers and looking up to read the time on

Woolworths clock tower, so that should give you an idea how low we were flying.

Bryan looked on the RAF as a second family, particularly thriving under those older men like Doc MacDonald, George Reid, Ack Greenwood and Owen Hooker, who combined steady and inspiring leadership with the ability to relax and have fun.

After the war, Bryan Wild trained at Kidderminster as a primary school teacher, specialising in art. He taught in Bolton, living with his Aunt Olive and then in digs, which he found rather depressing. After a time he wrote to Owen Hooker in New Zealand, who immediately replied in four foolscap sheets suggesting that Bryan should go out to New Zealand and stay with the Hookers for a while until accommodation was found and a new teaching career established. Bryan very nearly accepted his kind offer. However, he had other invitations. While at Bolton, Wild played wicket-keeper for Farnworth Cricket Club. Another player-member was the Bolton Wanderers and England footballer, Billy Moir, and in 1949 Billy invited Bryan to change his digs and move in with Moir and his wife—a much happier arrangement, especially for a Bolton Wanderers fan. Shortly after this, Bryan accepted a new teaching job in Newark, where Doc MacDonald and his wife were now living. He spent a few months with them until he found other accommodation, and it was there that he met his future wife, Bunty, at a dance in Nottingham.

Bryan and Bunty married in 1951. Doc MacDonald gave away the bride, as her father had just died, and Ron Pickles from 25 Squadron was best man. Bryan and Bunty had two children, Andrew and Elizabeth. Bryan followed his chosen career as a teacher, with a short break into furniture designing, ending up as Headmaster of Bestwood Primary School before his retirement.

Bryan kept in touch with both Doc MacDonald and Deryk Hollinrake throughout their lives. Deryk's daughter Jennifer is Bryan's Goddaughter. Bryan was stunned and delighted to discover in the 1990s that Joe Berry's widow, Joyce (now Joyce Manser) was living about six miles away from them near Nottingham. The friendship was resumed and now Bunty and Joyce are still in regular contact. Ralph Gibbons also lived fairly nearby, but Bryan never discovered it.

In his spare time Bryan painted in oils, acrylics and watercolours, specialising in ships, trains and, of course, aeroplanes. He painted every aircraft type he flew during the war. He also wrote three detective stories and a series of children's stories, none of them ever published. When he was younger he played amateur football and cricket, and continued to play chess at a high level until his mid-eighties, latterly against that implacable opponent, his chess computer.

Bryan Wild died on 21 January 2012 at the age of 90, after suffering from Parkinson's disease. To the end he was interested in aviation history and the connection to his wartime friends and experiences was very dear to him.

Flight Lieutenant W. K. 'Jack' Barnes

Jack Barnes survived the war and became a commercial pilot. No more is known of him at this time.

Flying Officer Richard 'Dicky' Bastow

Richard Bastow won no honours or awards but in his flying career he destroyed a Heinkel and a Ju 88, and probably damaged another enemy aircraft on the mission in which he died.

His first kill was 5 August 1942, with 125 Squadron, when he and his RO Sgt Clifford George managed to identify a Heinkell 111 against the moonlight and shoot it down in a ball of flame over the sea. Bastow and Sgt George then transferred to 600 Squadron in North Africa, and claimed a Ju 88 destroyed.

On the night of 14 May 1943 Dicky Bastow was on a dusk patrol with three other Beaufighters when, at 2130 hours, raids were reported thirty miles to the north of Bone. Four bandits were sighted, and Bastow reported one enemy aircraft damaged. He was pursuing another towards Bone when he reported that the guns were throwing all they had at him. The next that was heard of the encounter was that searchlights had picked up a Beaufighter close to a Ju 88, and the Beaufighter had crashed on the shore ten miles west of Cap de Garde. Dicky Bastow and Plt Off. Clifford George were killed. Both are buried at Bone War Cemetery, Annaba. Dicky Bastow was only 20 years old when he died.

Squadron Leader Joseph Berry DFC**

Joseph Berry was born on 28 February 1920, one of three children. He was brought up in Northumberland but left school at 16 and moved to Nottingham, where he worked in the Inland Revenue. There he met Joyce, whom he married in 1942, two years after enlisting.

Sqn Ldr Joseph Berry DFC shot down an unsurpassed record number of V1 bombers before being shot down and killed over Holland in October 1944. *Photograph courtesy of Graham Berry in 2013*

After completing his flying training he was posted to 256 Squadron, before flying to North Africa. Joe was awarded the DFC while in 255 Squadron. The citation reads:

> This officer is an exceptionally capable pilot who has destroyed three enemy aircraft in the course of a long and strenuous tour of duty. During operations at Salerno in September 1943 he shot a Junkers 88 down in flames, and on the following night destroyed a Messerschmitt 210 over the Italian coast. His third victory took place over Naples in October 1943 when he shot down another Ju 88. Flying officer Berry has been forced to abandon his aircraft on two occasions and has operated with coolness and courage in the face of heavy enemy action.

Ian Watson was also awarded the DFC for the same operations.

As Commanding Officer 501 Squadron, Joe came into his own flying the new single-seat Hawker Tempest in the battle against the flying bombs, a highly secret operation at the time in which he recorded the highest number of successes in destroying V1s in mid-flight on their route to London, and for this work he received the first Bar to DFC. V1s took the lives of over 6,000 and injured nearly 18,000 during the war. Later, as the Allies advanced through France, Joe Berry led two intruder sorties over Germany, and on 2 October 1944 was shot down near Veendam, Holland by an unlucky hit from small arms fire that ruptured the glycol tank. Eye witnesses reported that the plane gained height, presumably in order for the pilot to bale out, trailing glycol vapor behind it. Joe radioed to his fellow pilots, "Carry on chaps, I've had it" The plane crashed in flames in a small hamlet nearly five miles south of Scheemda. Two of the other pilots circled the crash site but it was obvious Joe could not survive such an impact. Some villagers rushed to the crashed plane and pulled the dead pilot from the blazing wreckage, desperately trying to extinguish the flames from his uniform. The identity tags were destroyed in the blaze, so Joe's identity was unknown, the only clue being a cigarette case with the initials JB on it.

Joseph was buried in Scheemda, under the epitaph of 'Unknown RAF Pilot', until much later research identified him. In 1999 Joe's widow, Joyce Berry (now Joyce Manser) and the rest of his family travelled to Scheemda where a new headstone had been erected and a fitting tribute was paid to Joseph's memory. The crash site of Joe's plane has been investigated and the larger parts of the plane which remained in the ground are now to be seen at the War museum in Uithuizen. There is an extant BBC recording of Joe talking about fighting the doodle-bugs, and at Eden Camp at Malton in North Yorkshire is a V1 bomber and display information about Joe.

Bruce the dog

Bryan Wild had to part with Bruce when he went into digs after the war, but saw him regularly, as Bruce moved in with Aunt Olive and lived a long and happy life. Reportedly Bruce always looked up intently into the sky at the sound of aeroplanes overhead.

Flight Sergeant Roger Colley

James Roger Colley was 22 years old when he died with Arthur Horsfall on 14 November 1943. He was known in 46 Squadron as Roger, but to his family as 'Robin'. Roger's father was a cobbler, a well-read, self-educated man who valued education for his two sons, David and 'Robin'. This was reflected in the possessions returned to the family when Robin died, which included two books of poetry and collected Shakespeare, Chaucer's *Canterbury Tales*, Virginia Woolf's *Death of the Moth and other Essays* and E. M. Delafield's *Diary of a Provincial Lady*, the last of which one hopes Roger enjoyed reading in the desert surroundings of North Africa. Like many relatives at the time, his family did not know the details about what had happened to their son; only that he was 'missing, presumed killed' in action. He is remembered on the Alamein Memorial.

Flight Lieutenant David James Crerar

David Crerar was born in 1922. He served in 219 Squadron at Tangmere in 1941, before being posted to 46 Squadron in 1942.

After being demobbed, David read English and History at Balliol College, Oxford. While at Oxford he met Eileen Chester Walsh, whom he married in 1949. David taught History at Clifton College, Bristol, until in 1952 he and Eileen moved to Irelend, where they had four children. They lived at Williamstown House, Castlebellingham, Co. Louth. After establishing a market garden, David set up a factory locally, Kay Brothers, manufacturing firelighters, which was eventually taken over by Reckitt & Colman. David was a keen horseman and was joint master of the Louth Hounds, and also continued flying as an instructor at a local airfield. He continued as a director of Reckett & Colman until his death.

In 1974, David and Eileen were tragically killed in a car accident while on holiday in the UK. An ironic twist was that Bill Howell, one of David's navigators during the war, was also killed in the same accident.

Squadron Leader William Arthur Cuddie

William Cuddie was born in Regina in Canada and educated at St Chad's College and at Victoria High School at Edmonton. He went to Britain to join the RAF in August 1939. After training he was posted 141 Squadron in August 1940, based in Scotland.

Here, at 22.35 hrs on the night of 10th May 1941, Bill Cuddie and his gunner were scrambled to intercept a Messerschmitt 110 which had been tracked from Northumberland to the West Coast of Scotland. Cuddie did not know that it was piloted by Rudolf Hess, Hitler's deputy, on a secret mission to land in Scotland and try and negotiate a peace deal with Germany. Cuddie got near to Hess's aircraft, possibly as close as four miles, but Hess baled out and parachuted into Eaglesham Moor, while his Me110 crashed nearby. Hess was captured, held, and tried after the war, finally committing suicide in Spandau Prison in 1987.

Bill Cuddie took part in the Battle of Britain, and served in Malta and North Africa before his death on 3 October 1943. He is still remembered by his wider family, where stories of the heroic 'Billy' Cuddie were common when they were young.

His body was never found, and he is commemorated in the Alamein Memorial.

David Crerar at his wedding to Eileen Chester Walsh in 1949. *Photograph courtesy Peter Crerar in 2013*

Flight Sergeant Ralph William Alfred George Gibbons

Ralph Gibbons was born in Norfolk in 1911, and had two younger sisters. He gained a BSc at Durham University, and in 1932 started teaching at Clay Cross Senior Boys' School, beginning a long career there which continued after the war. He became head of both the science and maths departments before becoming assistant headmaster. At the outbreak of war he was married to Annie with a young family. His eldest of three children, Ralph, recalls: 'One outstanding memory was that after the end of the war and before his demob, with his pilot, they 'shot up' our house on several occasions. At roof height this was quite an experience. We were always handed a bar of chocolate, carefully wrapped to survive being dropped from the Mosquito. It was years later that we found out that they were from a local shop and not from my dad!'

After parting from Bryan Wild on their return to Britain in April 1944, Ralph was trained as an instructor with 62 OTU in Northumberland, before becoming an instructor with 420 and 425 RCAF Squadrons at Tholthorpe in Yorkshire, which was operated by Bomber Command. In October 1944, he was posted to 1692 Bomber Support Training Unit at Great Massingham, Norfolk. Here he teamed up with Flying Officer McAlpine, with whom he moved to 23 Squadron, flying operationally at Little Snoring in Norfolk in November 1944 until he was demobbed in May 1945.

After the war, Ralph Gibbons spent twelve years as a warrant officer in the Clay Cross Territorial Unit. He continued a long association with Chesterfield and District Football Association, which had begun in 1932, standing as Chairman and for ten years as treasurer. Ralph Junior remembers also that his father had some kind of musical diploma from his time at university, and that he played the piano at school assemblies. Ralph Gibbons managed the Clay Cross Boys XI and several local district football clubs, and played an active role in the local darts league and Bestwood Working Men's Club. Bryan Wild and Ralph Gibbons lived relatively close to each other but remained unaware of the fact. Ralph died on 7 September 1996.

Sergeant Stanley Wheatley Greenwood

Stanley Greenwood was born on 7 September 1912. He enlisted on 18 August 1940 in Australia and embarked for the UK in April 1941. Ack's father lived in Hessle, Yorkshire, where Ack is buried: Comp. 53, Plot 13, Grave 1.

Ack Greenwood was not married, but within weeks of his death, earnest enquiries for information were made in Melbourne by a Miss Elsie Chambers, 'a personal friend of Sgt Greenwood', who had learned unofficially that Sgt Greenwood had been killed. She was not listed as among those to be informed of a casualty. She was told the date of the accident and the place of Stanley's burial, but not the cause. On 7 March 1942, Elsie Chambers wrote a letter to the RAF, asking for further information on the nature of the accident in which Greenwood died. It is not known what reply, if any, she received.

After the war was over, Bryan Wild sent a letter of condolence to Ack Greenwood's father, and later kept a photograph of Ack's gravestone in his album.

See also Plt Off. Olney, below.

Pilot Officer Peter Harrison-Yates

On 10 March 1943, P/O Harrison Yates was was flying a 256 Squadron Beaufighter at Woodvale with Sgt W. Patterson, when one of the engines failed fifty miles out to sea. Harrison-Yates nursed it back to land but had to crash-land on a sports field; Peter was killed but Sgt Patterson got away with slight injuries. Harrison-Yates was cremated at Anfield Crematorium, Liverpool.

Sergeant James Shepard 'Tex' Holland

Tex Holland was born in the USA but went to Canada to join the RCAF in order to join the war effort. He won the DFM in February 1943 when flying Wellington bombers with 70 Squadron in North Africa, one of few American pilots to be awarded that honour. His citation reads:

> Throughout his tour of bombing operations this airman has exhibited conspicuous gallantry and determination to reach and attack his target. On one occasion over Tobruk, when the front hatch of the aircraft was blown off by anti-aircraft fire, his coolness almost certainly saved the life of the navigator.
>
> On another occasion Sergeant Holland was detailed to attack the defences at Tobruk. He successfully bombed two heavy gun positions and a searchlight and subsequently made five runs just offshore machine-gunning searchlights.

On many other occasions this airman has given evidence of determination and tenacity in the face of enemy opposition which has been a source of inspiration to the squadron.

After his period with 46 Squadron Tex was posted to 227 Squadron in Libya. In December 1944 he went to Canada as an instructor until he was demobbed in August 1945. After the war, Tex set up a crop-spraying operation and in the mid-sixties set up a business travelling the world performing dare-devil flying tricks at air shows, such as flipping his plane upside down to cut a ribbon hung from a pole just five yards off the ground. He settled in St Augustine, Florida for the last thirty years of his life, where he died aged 89 in November 2006.

Warrant Officer Deryk Hollinrake

Deryk was one of seven children born and brought up on his parent's farm near Todmorden, West Yorkshire. Deryk never wanted to be a farmer, although horses and horse racing played a big part in his life after the RAF. Deryk was a keen and gifted footballer, playing in midfield for the Ferney Lee Flyers, Burnley FC and also the RAF.

In April 1939 when he enlisted as a wireless operator, and following his initial training, he was posted to Épernay in France with the Advanced Air Striking Force. After the German invasion of France he and his colleagues were forced to escape south, mainly on foot, arriving in Marseilles in June 1940 where they were able to find a ship which took them to Gibraltar and then on to Liverpool, arriving on 7 July 1940.

Deryk was then stationed at 256 Squadron, Squires Gate, Blackpool, where he met up with his good friends Ray Jeffs and Bryan Wild. On leaving Squires Gate he trained as a navigator/radio operator and was posted to Cranfield where he crewed up with Sid Trice. His next overseas posting was to 153 squadron at Surcouf in North Africa, flying with the North African Coastal Command. After covering the landings in Sicily, he was seconded as an instructor to the American Air Corps working with the Americans on the Beau night-fighter planes which had been supplied by the RAF. Following a number of operations with the Americans in Italy, Deryk was posted to India in February 1944 to undertake conversion work on Beaufighters with 176 Squadron. After contracting malaria, dysentery and shingles he was sent home in June 1944 and posted to Cranfield as an instructor where he met up again with Bryan Wild. Deryk finished his flying days on Mosquitos, which he loved, and was de-mobbed in December 1945.

During the war, Deryk lost two of his brothers who were both aircrew. Donald was shot down over Norway whilst supplying the resistance and Keith was killed on a night-flying test.

In August 1944 Deryk married June and they had two children, Jennifer and Andrew. In 1946 they bought a small shop which they built up and sold in 1949. After working with his father-in-law for five years he started a bookmaking business and became heavily involved in the horse-racing world, going on to own four racehorses over a number of years. After nearly twenty years Deryk sold the bookmaking business and bought an old inn on the moors above Todmorden. He retired in 1975. Deryk was a lover of good food and wine, which he passed on to his family and which he always attributed to that first RAF posting to the Champagne region around Épernay, France. Deryk died in 1992, aged 72.

Deryk never talked much about his life in the RAF; most of this information has come from letters written to old colleagues, and from his wife's memories.

Bryan Wild and Deryk were, in Bryan's words, 'the closest of friends', and they remained so for life.

Flight Lieutenant Cecil Owen Hooker

Owen Hooker was born on 22 August 1913 in New Plymouth, Auckland, New Zealand. He studied at Hamilton Technical College, and spent some time in farming, as well as volunteering with the Territorial Army before joining the police. Owen met Olga in Christchurch, where her father was the Chief Superintendent of Police. When the second world war broke out, Owen enlisted on 19 August 1941, marrying Olga before he went overseas.

Owen served in 29 Squadron before being posted to 46 Squadron in May 1942, serving in Malta and then at Idku, where he met Bryan Wild. After Bryan and Owen had both teamed up again in No. 51 OTU, Owen was posted to New Zealand on 19 March 1944, but did not leave Britain until 2nd October, spending two weeks at the end of September in No. 12 Personnel Despatch and Reception Centre in Brighton. It is not known where Owen was between March and September; a family rumour is that he flew Churchill at some stage, but so far it has not been possible to substantiate this.

On his return from overseas it was understood he wanted to stay in the air force after the war but Olga wanted him to stay at home, and in any case his age was against him. He returned to the police force and he and Olga had their family of seven children. At 45 years of age, he decided to go into farming, at which he was very successful. He finally suffered from a stroke, and a few years later died from a heart attack, in 1993. He is buried in the RSA cemetery in Morrinsville, and Olga's ashes were interred in the same plot.

What type of man was Owen? His family described him as very laid-back and quiet; often in family situations he wouldn't have a lot to say. On the other hand, he was a deep thinker and thought a lot about the world. In his farming he was very forward thinking. One of his innovations was what he called a loafing pad for the cows to stand on during the winter whilst feeding, instead of being on the waterlogged paddocks. Many modern New Zealand farmers now use this method.

He believed in education as a way out of the poverty trap, and was strongly in favour of equality, encouraging all his daughters to succeed in their chosen careers. His underlying driving force was his family, who always came first, and he immensely enjoyed all family activities. He was involved in his children's lives, supporting them in their choice of sport; he coached rugby school teams, and netball, taught swimming and helped run the school swimming sports. He was on the Parent Teachers Association. He himself was a good sportsman and loved games of all sorts, including board games and playing cards. He was chairman of the Motumaoho Hall Committee and also the bowls committee for a time. He played golf and snooker and was still riding his pushbike until his stroke intervened.

He didn't discuss the war much over the years, but he did tell a story once about flying over enemy territory at night and wondering why he was being fired on—till his mate told him his landing light was still on. On another occasion, his son David asked him, 'How come they made you Squadron Leader, Dad?' He answered, 'Because there was nobody else left.'

In Bryan Wild's log book is an entry from the time in 1944 that he and Owen were in 51 Operational Training Unit together. In later life Bryan has noticed that the entry for the signature of the officer commanding reads, 'Owen Hooker, F/Lt', and he has crossed it out and replaced it with 'S/Ldr'. The 'F/Lt' was what Bryan wrote in at the time, but the alteration in biro, with its slightly wobbly writing, is quite recent, probably written in Bryan's eighties. It shows that, as far as Bryan Wild's memory was concerned, Owen Hooker was his Squadron Leader—acting or otherwise. And ever more will be so.

Flight Lieutenant Joseph Arthur Horsfall

Three weeks before this book was to be submitted to the publishers, a diary of a second world war airman came to light in Canada, given to one

Tom Newell, an aviation enthusiast, by a friend who had purchased it ten years earlier in a box of old books from a garage sale. The diary had no name in the front, but from researching online and matching dates, places and names within it, including that of Bryan Wild, Tom Newell thought it might be that of Arthur Horsfall. It turned out to be the very five-year diary that Bryan Wild packed away with Arthur's belongings on 15 November 1943 in their tent in Idku, the day after Arthur died.

The diary entries are short memoranda of events and appointments rather than a descriptive account. But they mention the same people, places and happenings that Bryan Wild, on the other side of the tent, was writing about in his own diary: Jack Barnes, the Doc, Owen Hooker, and the 'haunts' of Alexandria, as well as brief notes on sorties, growing more frequent towards October and November of 1943. Of course, the last entry in Arthur's diary is 13 November 1943, when he spent the morning with a friend who visited the Mess that day.

In a postscript to Arthur's story, it is now known that he and Roger Colley were shot down by Ofhr Alexander Ottnad of 8 Staffel, his third victory; the fourth came over Leros on 16 November when he shot down a Beaufighter of 47 Squadron. Ottnad eventually went on to claim 24 Allied planes altogether, before he was wounded in action in June 1944 and shot down and captured (as a Leutnant, by this time) in the middle of August 1944.

Flight Sergeant Fred House

Fred House was killed in June 1942 when his Whitley V Bomber, P4944, which took off from Abingdon was shot down over Hamburg. Fred House and his other two British colleagues from the crew are commemorated on the Runnymede Memorial.

Sergeant Pilot Tommy Hunter

After returning to England from Moose Jaw and parting from Wild, Ward, and Wills, Sgt Plt Tommy Hunter was posted to 52 OTU and subsequently joined 263 Squadron at Filton in June 1941. The Squadron's Whirlwind fighters were concerned with protection of shipping over the Bristol Channel, and intruder patrols to attack aerodromes on the northern continent; difficult operations aggravated by the short range the Whirlwinds' petrol tanks allowed.

On 29 September 1941, Tommy Hunter took off at 18.33 from Predannack in P7009 with three other Whirlwinds, crossed the Channel at zero feet in murky weather, and arrived to attack Lannion aerodrome at 19.10.

The aerodrome was empty of the expected parked Ju 88s, and when the Whirlwinds went in to attack the few that were there, they were hit by an intense barrage of flak from all sides. Three Whirlwinds eventually returned home safely but reported seeing nothing of Tommy Hunter's plane through the murky darkness and tracer. One plane landed with only three gallons of petrol in the tank; another pilot force-landed by moonlight in a field when both engines failed within three seconds of each other, writing off the plane but walking away unscathed. Both these pilots had called Control to state that they might have to bale out.

Tommy Hunter also called Control, at 19.57, five miles from the coast with his engines failing. He thought he would bale out, but one minute later he called again and said he would not bale out until he was over the coast. Immediately after that, he called again, saying that he was baling out over the coast. Nothing more was heard or seen of him. Exeter Observer Corps reported that a pilot had been seen baling out over the sea five miles south west of the Eddystone Lighthouse at 2005 hrs. Extensive search and rescue operations over the next 48 hours over sea and land failed to find any trace of Tommy Hunter.

In his report, the CO highlighted the fact that three of the four aircraft had experienced similar problems on return to base, calling Control to say they were baling out. Tommy Hunter was indeed forced to bale out, and died as a result. At that stage, emergency dinghies were not standard issue for fighter pilots, who had to rely on Mae West life jackets to stay afloat in icy-cold water.

Tommy Hunter is commemorated at the Monk Helseden (Blackhall) Cemetery in Durham.

Squadron Leader William Kemp DSO DFC

Bill Kemp was born in Russell, North Auckland, New Zealand in 1915. He was working as an abattoir assistant when he enlisted at the age of 25, subsequently serving in the Middle East, North Africa and Europe. In an attack on enemy shipping in January 1944 with three other aircraft, his plane was hit by anti-aircraft fire which rendered all the electrical equipment unserviceable. Bill was badly injured in the foot from shrapnel but although he was in pain and losing a lot of blood he refrained from informing his leader of the injury and continued until all three ships were hit and set on fire, and then maintained formation throughout the homeward flight. His injury did not come to light until he was back at base. He was awarded the DFC for this sortie and his part in operations in North Africa.

Towards the end of the war Kemp applied for duties in the far East, where the war with Japan continued, but was instead made Commanding Officer of 487 Squadron RNZAF. He was awarded the DSO in September 1945 and appointed Air Attaché, Greece, in 1946. After the war he retired to Australia, where he pioneered crop spraying and advised the Australian Federal Government on the subject.

Squadron Leader Gilbert Alexander Muir

'Sheriff' Muir was a Canadian, born in 1912 in Winnipeg, where he was also raised and enlisted in the RCAF on 13 June 1941. Since he had worked on the long line test board of the Manitoba Telephone System before joining up, he was commissioned immediately in the Radio Branch Overseas, firstly to Britain in July 1942 and to the Middle East in December. He became special signals officer for 46 Squadron, and Wing Commander Reid was highly appreciative of Muir's expertise. As Reid writes in his operational record book summary for April 1943:

> F/Lt A G Muir, this unit's Canadian special signals officer, must take a lot of credit for the new type exercises in which, for the first time in the war, a Night Fighter was controlled by warships—HMS EURAYLUS AND HMS ORION—for the purpose of intercepting an aircraft at night. It was F/Lt Muir, too, who devised a 'Mother' beacon for the controlling ship which means a lot when doing air escort work on a dark night at any height.

On the night of the 5 March 1944, Muir's skills made a significant contribution to the success of Grp Capt. Max Aitken DSO DFC in destroying two enemy aircraft, probably destroying another and damaging one more. Muir was awarded the DFC effective from May 1944, in which month he was also promoted to Squadron leader. He retired from the RCAF in June 1945.

Flight Lieutenant Alistair Macdonald MBChB

Alistair 'Doc' MacDonald was born on 16 May, 1908, the youngest of three brothers. He initially attended Aberdeen Agricultural College, but later graduated in Medicine from Aberdeen University. After various

House jobs, during which he met and married Ida, he gained a partnership in a two-doctor practice in Newark, where his daughters Katharine and Margaret were born. At the outbreak of war he joined the RAF as a doctor, serving at home and abroad, and it was in the RAF where he met so many of his lifelong friends, including Bryan Wild, Terry Woods, Jack Barnes, Tommy Scade, Tom Rowland, Robbie (Shorus) Robertson, Harry Doodson, and Bish Martin. 46 Squadron was very special to the Doc and he himself embodied the special spirit of that Squadron. Bryan Wild and the Doc remained great friends throughout their lives. The Doc's eightieth-Birthday treat from his daughters was a two-hour flight on Concorde. Bryan drew him a cartoon in celebration of this event, showing Concorde landed in the desert and the Doc in flying jacket leaning against one of Concorde's tyres, with the caption, 'Don't tell me you made a forced landing in this one as well as a Tiger Moth!' Doc framed it and it always hung on his wall. Doc's ukulele is still in the family, inscribed with many signatures from 46 Squadron, including Bryan Wild's.

Pilot Officer William John Paterson Olney

Olney had had 330 hours' solo flying, 208 of which were in Defiants, before he crashed Defiant (Type I) No V116 on 7 February 1942, killing himself and air gunner Sgt Stanley 'Ack' Greenwood. The inquiry found that the aircraft was fit for flight and serviceable, and according to the report of the Commanding Officer, Grp Capt. H. D. Rogers, the cause of the accident was 'due to an error of judgement by the pilot when carrying out a steep turn at a very low altitude which was in direct contravention to local flying standing orders and the specific verbal instructions of the officer authorizing the flight.' The official 'Remarks of the Group Commander' were as follows:

> I agree that this accident resulted from disobedience of orders on the part of the pilot who was experienced and well qualified to carry out the exercise. The Squadron concerned will not be permitted to take part in such exercises in future.

The Officer Commanding, Group Captain J. A. McDonald, reported,

> I agree generally with the findings. During an exercise of this nature low flying is permissible since the exercise cannot be carried out without low flying. Standing Orders do not apply to exercises for which special instructions and/or operational orders are issued.

P/O Olney clearly disregarded both the orders given to him before flight and his leader's instructions during the exercise.

Pilot Officer Olney is remembered on the Runnymede Memorial.

Flight Lieutenant Wilfred Robert Peasley DFC

Bob Peasley gained the DFC and survived the war. He married Anne Lawrence Mott in 1946, with whom he had three daughters.

Flying Officer Rhys Trevor 'Charlie' Peace

Charlie Peace's body was never found, and no account was given of the manner of his death.

He is remembered with honour in the Alamein Memorial.

Pilot Officer Kurt Kenneth Keston Pelmore

Keston Pelmore was born in Peterborough in 1911. In 1936 his love and enthusiasm for Bentley cars led him to found a Club for Bentley owners, which, apart from a gap for the war years, has thrived and continued until the present day.

At the outbreak of war he returned to England from America, but at 28 he was initially considered too old to enlist. He took a desk job with the Admiralty until he eventually enlisted in July 1940. He trained at 13 Elementary Flying Training School in August before going to Moose Jaw and gaining his wings. On returning to the UK he was sent north to No. 2 Operational Training Unit at Lossiemouth before being posted to 101 Squadron Oakington (Bomber Command). He flew eighteen missions as pilot on Vickers Wellingtons in campaigns over North West Europe. Sadly, on 27 December 1941, Keston Pelmore died with the rest of his crew when his Wellington bomber was shot down on a mission to Düsseldorf. In commemoration of this remarkable and talented person, the Bentley Drivers Club in 2013 organised a trip to the site in Germany where his Wellington crashed, and to the Rheinhardt Cemetery, where Keston is buried along with his crew.

Flight Lieutenant Kenneth Gordon Rayment

Ken Rayment was born on 11 March 1921 in Wanstead, Essex. He joined up in 1940, and like Wild, trained at Moose Jaw in 1941 (on a later course) where he passed out top of his course. After being commissioned he went to Sutton Bridge, 56 OTU, in September 1941 and was posted to 153 Squadron in December. He won the DFC in North Africa, and returned to the UK in April 1944 before posting to 264 Squadron. His wartime record claimed six destroyed, one damaged and one V1 destroyed. Kenneth continued flying commercially after the war, on Oxfords, Dakotas, Vikings and Ambassadors, becoming a senior captain. Famously, on 6 February 1958 he was second pilot and—controversially—at the controls on the fated flight from Munich carrying the Manchester United team, which, after two aborted take-offs crashed on the third attempt, killing 23 people. Kenneth Rayment survived the crash but his head and internal injuries were severe. After some time his leg was amputated but he never regained consciousness and died on 15 March 1958.

Wing Commander George Alfred Reid

George Alfred Reid was born in Arnprior, Ontario, Canada on 12 August 1907. He was educated at St Andrew's College, Aurora, where he was head boy, graduating in 1927. He played many sports, including boxing, cross country, rugby and cricket, playing for the School's first team in both. He was described as 'a fair left bat but a good right hand slow bowler.' He studied at Stamford University in California, and Edinburgh University (1931). He was 32 when he enlisted in April 1939, ending up in 603 (City of Edinburgh) Squadron. After some time as a flying instructor in Britain, he arrived in HQ RAF Middle East in March 1942 and was posted to 46 Squadron on 4 May that year, when after a long period of inactivity, the Squadron moved to Idku and reformed as a night-fighter squadron with Beaufighters.

Throughout August 1942 the planes of 46 Squadron were busy, bombing and strafing roads and transport while Rommel's army retreated, and then in a Coastal Command capacity, escorting shipping convoys. Towards the middle of the month, Reid led an attachment to Malta, which included Flg Off. Hooker, who remained until 28 December. Reid meanwhile moved to Benghazi to oversee the establishment of a new detachment there, where, on 14 August, a convoy of twenty-six vehicles arrived by road, carrying approximately 150 personnel comprising Maintenance and 'B' Flights. Wing Commander Reid shot down a Ju 88 on 22 August 1942, suffering aircraft damage from return fire.

In Alexandria in late 1942, George Reid met and married an English girl, Rosemary Campion. They lived in Alexandria where she carried out decoding work for the Allies.

It cannot have been an easy task to manage the rather chaotic formation of the Squadron in the Middle East at this time. Personnel were coming and going in large numbers, and detachments in Abu Sueir, Benghazi and St Jean in Palestine meant that administration had to be carried out over a wide area. But Reid was a capable organiser, and it is evident that the Spirit of 46 was formed largely through the open, friendly, charming, and affectionate style of its commanding officer, one who was at the forefront of the effort on the ground and the fight in the air, and who revelled in giving praise and credit to those around him where it was due. Bryan Wild considered him to be one of the most inspiring and enabling leaders he ever knew.

The spirit of George Reid perhaps best comes across in the language of his monthly summaries of events in the 46 Squadron operational record books. The Summary for June begins, delightfully, 'In the early days of this month with new crews arriving as fast as the flowers were fading...' It continues with lively accounts of successful operations. Reid's Summary for July 1943 paints a vivid and nostalgic picture of one day's entertainment:

> The event of July, and one which brought to some of us memories of better days in better lands, was 46 Squadron Sports Day.... in good old English style.
>
> Altogether it was a great day, with some keen inter-section competition for the shield which finally went to Signals section, with the officers, to their shame, finishing at the lowest end of the table. It was even a day out for the natives on the camp, as wheedled into activity by the blandishments of W/O Meager they took part in an All-Egyptian 200 yards ... for one moment we had hopes of seeing some healthy competition from Sgt Barker, but after a trial spurt he gave up the idea.
>
> Ice cream at the tea-interval was another of those surprises which make life so much the sweeter. Let's hope that next year's sports day will see strawberries and cream—somewhere in England.

Reading these accounts, it is easy to understand why Bryan Wild and others in the Squadron held Reid in such affection, and always remembered 3 October 1943, the day when he was shot down, along with other friends, as 'Black Sunday'.

Squadron Leader T. P. K. Scade, DFC

Tommmy Scade resigned his rank of Wing Commander in August 1946. After the war he returned to his native Kenya with his wife Vivienne, and was visited on at least one occasion by Doc MacDonald.

Flight Lieutenant Donovan Toone

Donald Toone and Flg Off. Hutchings in Beaufighter V8457 were reported missing 15 miles west of Blackpool whilst on a night-training exercise on 9 February 1943. It is believed Toone may have lost control in turbulent cloud in the midst of a hailstorm. No trace was found of the missing Beaufighter.

Flight Lieutenant Jimmy Ward

In Bryan Wild's photograph album he wrote underneath a photograph of Jimmy Ward in Moose Jaw, 'Died, 1945', but he knew nothing more than that. In fact, he was both wrong and, sadly, right about Jimmy's fate.

Jimmy Ward was posted from 456 Squadron to 255 Squadron on 9 September 1942 and went with 255 to North Africa. Jimmy Ward was made Acting Flight Lieutenant in January 1944 and returned to the UK from the Middle East in the Spring of that year. Contrary to Bryan Wild's information, he survived the war, and continued his career with the RAF. But on 17 November 1952, Jimmy Ward died in an air accident off the coast of Sunderland, in which his Meteor NF11 aircraft broke up and exploded in mid-air at about 800 feet, and crashed into the sea. His body and that of his navigator were never found. At the time, Jimmy was an instructor at Central Flying School, and was at 228 Operational Training Unit undertaking a jets conversion course. He had 3,322 hours experience on all aircraft types, and had a School assessment of 'Above Average'. The subsequent court of inquiry was unable to establish the primary cause of the crash and therefore no blame was apportioned. The aircraft was virtually brand new and had previously handled without problems. No distress call was heard. Air accident investigation was rudimentary at that time, and no doubt opportunities were lost to establish in which area of the aircraft the failure was initiated. There was an eye-witness who commended the pilot for steering the doomed aircraft away from the town and towards the sea.

Flight Lieutenant James Ward was survived by his widow, Agnes 'Sue' Ward, who was still living in Heswall, Cheshire at the time of the accident, and two children.

Group Captain Bernard Wills DSO DFC

David Bernard Wills was born on 16 April 1922 at Wirral in Cheshire, and educated at Wallasey Grammar School.

His career in the RAF was a long and distinguished one, retiring as a Group Captain in January 1969. His wartime citation reads:

> Flight Lieutenant David Bernard Wills, RAFVR, No 68 Squadron. This officer is now on his second tour of duty. During his first tour he met with a serious accident but, with great determination, he was able to resume flying within a year. Since then as a deputy flight commander, Flight Lieutenant Wills has displayed great organizing ability, enthusiasm and devotion to duty and by his fine fighting spirit he has set an inspiriting example to all. He has destroyed at least three enemy aircraft.

The accident mentioned was between two Beaufighters, on 28 May 1944. Wills' Beaufighter was shot down when the guns of another aircraft were fired in error during a camera gun practice. Bernard Wills was badly injured and Flt Lt 'Peter' Ledeboer died later from his injuries.

Bernie Wills' first fighting 'kill' was with 456 Squadron in May 1942: a Ju 88. He also claimed a He 177 in June 1943 after being posted to 68 Squadron. On 3 March 1945, seventy German bombers crossed the English coast on their way to bomb the Midlands, and 68 Squadron Mosquitos were scrambled to intercept. In this sortie Bernard Wills shot down a Ju 188, which crashed into the sea in flames.

At the end of the war Bernie stayed with the RAF until his retirement, flying numerous jet fighter types from Meteors to Lightnings. He was Fighter Controller in Malta in the early 1950s and on exchange with the RCAF at St Hubert Montreal for three years. Bryan Wild would have been interested to learn that from 1960 to 1961 he commanded 46 Squadron flying Javelins, and then also 23 Squadron flying Javelins from 1962 to 1963. After suffering a heart attack whilst at the Air War college in Alabama Bernie returned to work as the CO at RAF Manston in 1965. He retired as a Wing Commander but was promoted to Group Captain as Air Commandant for the ATC South West division.

Bernie Wills married Shirley (a WAAF radar controller) in 1943 and had two sons, Timothy and Nigel. He died in December 1977 at the age of 56.

Bibliography

Argyle, C. *Chronology of World War II*. (London: Marshall Cavendish Books Ltd, 1980).

Air 27/ Squadron Operational Record Books for Squadrons 25, 46, 68, 89, 153, 227, 256, 456.

Bamford, J., *Eyes of the Night: The Air Defence of North-Western England 1940–1943*. (Barnsley: Pen & Sword Aviation, 2005).

Cull, B., *Fighters over the Aegean: Hurricanes over Crete, Spitfires over Kos Beaufighters over the Aegean, 1943–44*. (London: Fonthill Media, 2012).

Rogers, A., *Churchill's Folly: Leros and the Aegean*. (London: Cassell Military Paperbacks, 2004).

St Andrew's College *Review* collection, available online.

National Archives of Australia A705 Casualty reports.

Service records, Library and Archives Canada.

Cenotaph records database, Auckland War Memorial Museum.

London Gazette online archive.